D1331562

SMYTH   ‍LIBRARY

THE FILMS

COMPOSING FOR THE FILMS

Theodor Adorno and Hanns Eisler

With a new Introduction by Graham McCann

continuum

Continuum
The Tower Building   80 Maiden Lane
11 York Road   Suite 704
London   New York
SE1 7NX   NY 10038

www.continuumbooks.com

First published in 1947 by Oxford University Press, New York
This edition published 2007

British Library Cataloguing in Publication Data
A catalogue record for this book is available from the British Library

ISBN-13: 9780826499028
ISBN-10: 0826499023

Library of Congress Cataloging in Publication Data
A catalog record for this book is available from the Library of Congress

Typeset by BookEns Ltd, Royston, Herts.
Printed and bound in China by 1010 Printing International Ltd.

781.542
n 66/99

Contents

New Introduction
Graham McCann

And just because he's human
A man would like a little bite to eat.
He won't get full on a lot of talk
That won't give him bread and meat.

Brecht/Eisler[1]

Today it goes without saying that
nothing concerning art goes without
saying, much less without thinking.

Adorno[2]

Hollywood, 1943: Alfred Hitchcock's new movie, *Lifeboat*, is in production at 20th Century-Fox studios. The composer discovers one day that the director has decided against using any music in the movie. Puzzled, suddenly insecure, and a little angry, the composer asks why such an unusual change of mind has occurred. 'Well,' he is told, 'Hitchcock feels that since the entire action of the film takes place in a lifeboat on the open ocean, where would the music come from?' The composer sighed, shrugged his shoulders, gave a world-weary smile and replied: 'Ask Mr Hitchcock to explain where the camera came from, and I'll tell him where the music comes from.'

Music remains the least appreciated, and most overlooked, aspect of the medium of movies. It is still, for the most part, unspoken for. *Composing for the Films*, when it was first published in 1947, was a unique and challenging contribution to the theoretical and practical under-standing of the nature, and potential, of commercial movies and their musical scores. Today, fifty years after Hanns Eisler and Theodor Adorno began their remarkable project, the book continues to stand alone as an intelligent analysis of the social, political and aesthetic significance of movie music. One may disagree with some of its arguments, but one can still appreciate the rare critical respect it shows to a subject seldom taken seriously. It is concise but ambitious, boldly suggestive, a richly enticing overture. Its co-authors, Eisler and Adorno, represent two of the most significant traditions in twentieth century Marxism: Eisler Brechtian artistic practice, Adorno Critical Theory. Neither author recognized rigid disciplinary boundaries; as a consequence, to read *Composing for the Films* is to engage with aesthetic, economic, sociological, political and philo-sophical issues and concerns. It is, in the circumstances, a surprisingly lucid book.

Hanns Eisler (1898–1962), according to one of his biographers, 'paved the way for a social art in a field which today is still considered rather as a refuge from politics'.[3] He was born in Leipzig, but brought up in Vienna. His father was the Austrian philosopher Rudolf Eisler and his mother Marie Ida Fischer. He was the youngest of three children, his brother and sister becoming professional revolutionaries in Berlin. In 1919 he embarked on composition studies as the student of Karl Weigl at the New Viennese Conservatory. It was not long before he tired of Weigl's conventional, undemanding instruction, and, in spite of his lack of financial means, began a four-year period of private tuition with Arnold Schönberg, who waived his fee. It was an extraordinarily propitious time to be accepted into Schönberg's master class, coinciding as it did with the transition from atonal to twelve-tone composition. After Webern and Berg, Eisler was the first to write in the new technique.

His political radicalism caused him to clash with Schönberg, and, in 1925, after an intense period of debate and rebellion, he moved to Berlin to pursue his search for a new form of socialist music. He wrote direct yet musically sophisticated songs for communist choirs and agit-prop shows. As a militant composer he was to write several of the most outstanding songs of the international Communist movement, including the very familiar *Kominternlied (Comintern Song)*, *Lob des Lernens (In Praise of Learning)* and *Einheitsfrontlied (United Front Song)*. Strongly influenced by Bertolt Brecht's ideas on politically engaged art, he composed numerous theatre pieces and cantatas for texts by Brecht, in addition to incidental music for plays by Clifford Odets, Brecht and George Bernard Shaw. He began composing for movies in the late 1920s, working with such figures of pre-Hitler German culture as Waiter Ruttman *(Opus III,* 1927) and Slatan Dudow *(Kuhle Wampe,* 1931). His left-wing political associations made his eventual departure from Germany inevitable.

In the early 1930s he headed a short-lived International Music Bureau in Moscow, and worked in Vienna, Prague, Paris, London and Copenhagen before emigrating to the United States of America. After the war he was deported, settling first in Vienna and then, from 1950 until his death, in East Berlin, where he led a master class in composition at the Academy of the Arts and composed a number of proletarian-nationalist works for large choral groups, including the *Deutsche Sinfonie* of the German Democratic Republic.

Theodor Wiesengrund Adorno (1903–1969) was once described as 'Germany's most prominent academic teacher and an outstanding citizen of the Western European avant-garde'.[4] He was born in Frankfurt am Main, the only child of a wealthy and assimilated Jewish businessman, Oskar Wiesengrund, and his Catholic wife, Maria Calvelli-Adorno della Piana, a singer of Corsican and originally Genoese descent (the son's decision, on the brink of exile in 1938, to replace his patronymic Wiesengrund in favour of his mother's maiden name was made on the advice of his colleagues).[5] Precocious musically and intellectually, in 1921 he took courses at the Johann Wolfgang Goethe University in philosophy, sociology, psychology and music, emerging in 1924 with a doctorate in philosophy. He arrived in Vienna the following year to study music with Alban Berg. It was natural, given his talent and his mother's family connections, that Adorno should also establish personal ties with Schönberg, Webern, Krenek, Steuermann, Kolisch and other representatives of the modern school. He remained closest, however, to Berg, who seemed, to Adorno, a composer situated in between the modernity of Schönberg and the nostalgia of Mahler.[6] Although in 1927 he returned to Frankfurt to resume his academic studies, he retained close ties with Vienna, editing the influential journal *Anbruch* from 1928 to 1932.

His university teaching post at the University of Frankfurt, which he had taken up in 1931, grew increasingly precarious after the Nazi seizure of power in 1933. The rise of fascism changed the course of many European intellectuals' lives and careers, and Adorno, like Eisler, was no exception. Reluctantly, he had to leave his homeland. He would reflect, for the rest of his career, on the 'damaged lives' of himself and his fellow refugees. He went into temporary exile in Oxford, at Merton College, before joining the Institute of Social Research in New York.

The Institute had been established in Frankfurt in 1923, with classical Marxism as the theoretical basis of its programme, but had undergone a radical change in outlook in 1930 when the philosopher Max Horkheimer, an old friend of Adorno's, took over as its director.[7] In contrast to the ahistorical, scientistic Marxism associated with the Party, which seemed to discourage prudential forms of political theory, Horkheimer's Institute proposed a Marxism that was true to Marx's original, critical project: a theory *for* the times, a theory that changed *with* the times. The Institute's reanimated Marxism was thus a 'Critical Theory', radically opposed to dogmatism of any kind, constantly on guard against the twin dangers of fetishizing the general or the particular. The Institute was now committed to a programme of interdisciplinary study, explicating the set of mediations which enable the reproduction and transformation of society, economy, culture and consciousness.

The Institute was ideally suited to Adorno's prodigious and heterodox talents. He became the dominant intellectual influence on most of the Institute's research projects, both during the American exile and after the return to Frankfurt at the end of the forties (when he became its new director). He remained a resolute defender of the idea of 'nicht mitmachen', not playing along, a refusal to compromise in the name of practical expediency.[8] His thought resisted the temptation to countenance any premature resolution or reconciliation, seeking to preserve the dialectical unity of part and whole, particular and universal. He once wrote that, 'The dialectic advances by ways of extremes, driving thoughts with the utmost consequentiality to the point where they turn back on themselves, instead of qualifying them'.[9] His style was to brush against the grain of conventional thought, employing provocative exaggerations and ironic inversions to bring contradictions into bold relief: 'the value of a thought', he remarked, 'is measured by its distance from the continuity of the familiar'.[10]

'Refugees', wrote Bertolt Brecht, 'are the keenest dialecticians. They are refugees as a result of changes and their sole object of study is change. They are able to deduce the greatest events from the smallest hints. ... When their opponents are winning, they calculate how much their victory has cost them; and they have the sharpest eyes for contra-dictions.'[11] European immigration had reached its peak by 1941. Six hundred and thirteen displaced academics entered the United States between 1933 and 1945 under a rule giving exemption from the quota to any *émigrés* who had taught during the previous two years and had a guaranteed American teaching position. The Emergency Committee In Aid of Displaced Foreign Scholars found places for 459 of them; 167 settled at the 'University in Exile', set up by the New School for Social Research in New York. Eisler arrived there early in 1938, teaching a number of courses on music. In terms of numbers, the New School was by far the most important academic centre for *émigré* scholars in the U.S. It was not, however, the only significant institution associated with *émigré* intellectuals at that time.[12] In 1934 Columbia University provided a North American home for the Frankfurt Institute of Social Research. In its new location in New York's Morningside Heights Park, the Institute, under the direction of Horkheimer and characterized by the work of such figures as Adorno (who arrived later than the others, in the February of 1938), Franz Neumann, Leo Löwenthal and Herbert Marcuse, continued its self-consciously interdisciplinary theoretical investigations into the nature and causes of political totalitarianism.

Adorno, more so than any of his Institute colleagues, felt ill-at-ease in his new surroundings. 'Every intellectual in emigration', he was later to write, 'is, without exception, mutilated, and does well to acknowledge it to himself, if he wishes to avoid being cruelly apprised of it behind the tightly-closed doors of his self-esteem.'[13] Although he joined the other Institute members in acquiring American citizenship, he never entertained the possibility of settling there. Indeed, Leo Löwenthal later recalled that Adorno had been so slow to join his fellow critical theorists in America that 'we had to drag him almost physically'.[14] He considered himself 'European through and through', and regarded himself as such 'from the first to the last day abroad, and never denied it'.[15] One of his new colleagues observed: 'He looks as you would image a very absent-minded German professor, and he behaves so foreign that I feel like a member of the Mayflower society.'[16] Eisler was also uncomfortable with many aspects of the U.S., but, early on, he was more preoccupied with the fact of his chronic lack of money. Joris Ivens, with whom Eisler had collaborated on *Die Jugend hat das Wort* in 1932, now was President of the Association of Documentary Film Producers in New York, and Eisler hoped to receive some commissions for film music. He soon developed a network of supportive friends and potential patrons.

While most European academics found New York a congenial place to work, other *émigrés* found themselves, through either poverty or curiosity, drawn to the West Coast, to California. Adorno would move to Santa Monica, near Los Angeles, in 1941, when his colleague Horkheimer's uncertain health necessitated a warmer climate. Eisler would go there in 1942, hoping, among other things, to resume his collaboration with Brecht. They were joined by some unexpected guests. The European Film Fund, set up in Hollywood by several *émigré* movie makers at the end of 1939, had started to find minor jobs at the studios for distinguished immigrants so as to justify their continued presence in California. An elderly historian, for example, found himself working as a 'researcher' for a costume drama, and a musicologist was obliged to take a position as an apprentice to an undistinguished movie composer. In time, the strategy was extended to accommodate the new arrivals. As part of the belated rescue effort, the Hollywood studios Metro-Goldwyn-Mayer and Warner Brothers, prompted by the European Film Fund, had offered the Emergency Rescue Committee more than seventy 'blank' contracts as proof that the prospective immigrant could work. A strikingly varied group of poets, novelists, dramatists, musicians and artists arrived in Hollywood at the beginning of the 1940s, drawing token salaries of $100 per week and contemplating, with varying degrees of apprehension, a new, and perhaps permanent, career in the movies. Among those chosen for this assistance were Alfred Döblin, Walter Mehring, Alfred Neumann, Bertolt Brecht, Heinrich Mann, Ludwig Marcuse and Ernst Lothar. Of this group, only Brecht appeared to make a determined, if profoundly cynical, attempt to succeed in the novel environment.

Brecht described Hollywood as the 'centre of the international narcotics trade'.[17] He had few genuine friends among the *émigré* population, and he looked on with dismay as many of them settled into either a self-destructive misanthropy or a submissive materialism. Eisler met Brecht again, soon after the latter's arrival in Santa Monica, at the house of Adorno. For the five previous years their only contact with each other had been by correspondence, The reunion inspired them both. Eisler helped revive Brecht's spirits. When he resumed his working relationship with Eisler once more, Brecht noted that it felt 'a bit as if I am stumbling around muddle-headedly in some crowd and suddenly hear my old name called'.[18]

Neither artist, however, could afford to devote much of his time to their joint projects. Brecht wrote, in his poem *Hollywood*, of the need to 'go to the market' each morning, 'where they buy lies', in order 'to earn my bread'. He could find few suitable collaborators at the studios; those writers who regarded themselves as communists or fellow travellers were largely under the spell of Russian theatre and, in particular, the ideas of Stanislavsky. It was not easy for Brecht and Eisler to maintain their shared vision, their sense of a common artistic and political strategy. Eisler, in particular, was moving closer again to his old teacher Schönberg (Eric Bentley[19] recalls seeing the two men together at the time, Schönberg 'motionless, unsmiling', Eisler 'flitting about him with rapid gestures and broad smiles and a flood of flattering words') and was looking to concentrate more than before on his chamber and orchestral music. He was also obliged, in order to earn a living, to write a number of movie scores for the studios.

The group with which Eisler and Brecht associated was rather different from the larger refugee community in two basic ways: it was composed primarily of artists, and the politics of the group in general emphasized a more distinctively left-wing and activist anti-fascism. It was common at this time for many of the most distinguished *émigrés* to socialize together on Sunday afternoons, often at the Santa Monica home of Salka Viertel, at 165 Mabery Road. Viertel, a former actor and writer, had lived in the U.S. since 1927, was a close friend of Greta Garbo and Charlie Chaplin, and her home became a kind of salon for her artistic and political friends and acquaintances. It was an extraordinary meeting place for an extraordinary group of artists: actors Peter Lorre and Luise Rainer; conductor Otto Klemperer; composers Max Steiner, Dimitri Tiomkin, Bronislaw Kaper and Erich Korngold; directors William Dieterle, Fritz Lang, Emst Lubitsch and Billy Wilder; and writers Thomas and Heinrich Mann. In this odd society, unexpected friendships were forged, and unlikely alliances arranged. It was here, for example, that Charles Laughton befriended Brecht and Eisler, resulting in a collaboration on the first production of *Galileo*[20] and, less successfully, the hiring of Eisler as Laughton's German accent coach for the undistinguished movie *Arch of Triumph* (1948). It was here that Adorno and Thomas Mann would sometimes discuss the work-in-progress that would later become *Doctor Faustus* (1947), a novel marked, as Mann acknowledged, by 'brazen snatches' of Adorno's essays on the philosophy of music.[21] It also was here that Schönberg and Adorno would meet, as would, on occasion, an eclectic range of theatrical and musical figures, such as Clifford Odets, Stella Adler and Harold Clurman, Max Reinhardt and Christopher Isherwood, Artie Shaw and Ava

Gardner, Igor Stravinsky, Vladimir Horowitz, Vincent Price, Lion Feuchtwanger and Orson Welles.

In Viertel's memoir of the period, *The Kindness of Strangers*, she notes how Eisler found it much easier than Brecht to establish friendships at these meetings. Eisler, she remarks, was 'already acclimatized to Hollywood', his 'brilliant mind and jolliness' helping to make him a popular figure in American literary circles. Brecht, she recalls, was by far the more reserved of the two, appearing aloof and reticent because he 'refused to express himself stumblingly in an alien tongue', in stark contrast to Eisler, 'who, unconcerned about grammar and his atrocious accent, enlivened the dullest parties'.[22]

It was Salka Viertel who introduced Charlie Chaplin to Brecht and Eisler. Chaplin was rather suspicious of what he saw as Brecht's tendency to theorize systematically but at times obtusely about art, while Brecht, in turn, treated Chaplin with unusually 'cordial, attentive respect'. Eisler's relationship with Chaplin was noticeably warmer: Eisler had always regarded Chaplin as one of the most accomplished screen actors in the world, and Chaplin would later, in his autobiography, describe Eisler as a 'great musician'.[23] In 1946, Eisler acted as musical adviser on Chaplin's *Monsieur Verdoux* (1947). He wrote excitedly to Clifford Odets of his early experiences at the studio:

> Charlie has begun work here; he made a number of extended rushes and I watched him directing – his mastery is truly fantastic. Not only does he demonstrate to his actors what he wants but also what he does not want. He writes very good scenes, but naturally he is no author and often certain weaknesses and naive pseudophilosophical observations are unquestionably bad ... But these are only small faults, and taken as a whole what he is making is really a masterpiece. He has very rudimentary notions about music and composes vocal numbers and songs himself which do not please me at all. I don't see how I could work with him. But he is a marvellous chap and it is always a pleasure to spend an evening with him.[24]

Eisler came to believe that he and Brecht had radicalized Chaplin, and he regarded, rather grandly, the sharply ironic comic moments in *Monsieur Verdoux* as evidence of their influence.

Eisler's own, direct, experience of movie-making in Hollywood, however, was, in general, much less satisfying. As a musician, his position seemed particularly insecure. The *émigré* writers, although they found many aspects of Hollywood and the studio system difficult to comprehend, knew enough about popular fiction and commercial cinema to appreciate what was expected of them (even if they chose not to supply it). For European musicians, on the other hand, Hollywood bore scant relationship to anything that they had known in Germany or Austria. Few European movie producers chose to immerse a drama in the kind of all-enveloping score that was, it seemed, common to American cinema. Ernst Krenek, after a brief, near farcical, meeting with Sam Goldwyn, retreated to the East Coast to teach at Vassar. Arnold Schonberg, apart from a brief flirtation with the movie studios, established himself as a teacher at UCLA. Eisler, on the other hand, although he found a teaching post at the University of Southern California, had to come to terms with commercial cinema.

Eisler composed a number of scores for commercial movies, including (in collaboration with Brecht) Fritz Lang's *Hangmen Also Die* (1943), Clifford Odets' *None But the Lonely Heart* (1944), Frank Borzage's *The Spanish Main* (1945), Gustav Machate's *Jealousy* (1945), Harold Clurman's *Deadline at Dawn* (1946), Douglas Sirk's *A Scandal in Paris* (1946), Jean Renoir's *The Woman on the Beach* (1947) and Edward Dmytryk's *So Well Remembered* (1947). They were not, for Eisler, particularly rewarding or encouraging experiences. Even his contribution to the more openly political *Hangmen Also Die,* which attracted an Oscar nomination for Eisler, was marred by the bitter arguments between the director, Fritz Lang, Bertolt Brecht and his co-writer John Wexley over screen credits. If Brecht was increasingly frustrated by the compromises forced on him by the studios, Eisler, even though he lacked his friend's obstinacy, sometimes still found the lowly status accorded to the composer intolerable.

Eisler was, from the beginning, startled by the difficult conditions in which musicians and composers were expected to work. The movie studios had developed their own music departments. From their composers they required the simplest thread of a tune, which their arrangers could then expand into a score appropriate to the musicians available and the overall 'house style'. The studio composer, Eisler noted, needed ca kind of blue-print in mind, a framework which he must fill in at each given place and only then see to it that the fillings are vivid and striking'.[25] Because the completed score could subsequently be disturbed and distorted by the director's cuts, the composer had to develop a talent for 'planned improvisation', anticipating such hazards within the very structure of the score.[26] The studios thus favoured those composers who were capable of producing music to order, with a fluency and speed seldom, if ever, required elsewhere.

It was through such painful experiences that Eisler became the most articulate, and passionate, critic of movie music. In *Composing for the Films* he railed against the 'often grotesque artistic incompetence' of the music department heads, and the lowly status accorded to the composer.[27] He reflected on the individual composer's insecure position in the department, warning against both the lazy compromise and the proud but destructive act of defiance; both attitudes, he stressed, 'would only manifest his impotence'. Eisler also attacked the rigid structure of movie orchestras (confined by union agreement to a strict number of strings, woodwinds and brass), the wide spread practice of farming-out orchestration, and the habit of handing conducting duties to popular 'celebrity' performers or to mediocre orchestra players. He had some sympathy for the musicians themselves, forced to tolerate 'unworthy and often unendurably shabby cinema scores', a demanding studio regime 'that combines senseless pedantry with irresponsible bungling', inadequate conductors, and, the stress that came from the need to work long hours to complete a scene followed by weeks of unproductive idleness. Such working conditions, Eisler argued, encouraged carelessness and indifference, and an attitude of 'silent contempt toward the whole business'.[28]

What most exercised Eisler was the programmatic structure of the music they were obliged to play:

> There is a favorite Hollywood gibe: "Birdie sings, music sings". Music must follow visual incidents and illustrate them either by directly imitating them or by using clichés that are associated with the mood and content of the picture ... Mountain peaks invariably invoke string tremolos punctuated by a signal-like horn motif. The ranch to which the virile hero has eloped with the sophisticated heroine is accompanied by forest murmurs and a flute melody. A slow waltz goes along with a moonlit scene in which a boat drifts down a river lined with weeping willows ... When the scene is laid in a Dutch town, with its canals, windmills, and wooden shoes, the composer is supposed to send over to the studio library for a Dutch folk song in order to use its theme as a working basis.[29]

Arnold Schönberg had experienced this kind of humiliation at first hand. Irving G. Thalberg, the vice-president in charge of production at Metro-Goldwyn-Mayer studios, had asked Schönberg to compose a score, to be reminiscent of his early, 'lovely' music, for the movie version of Pearl Buck's Chinese saga *The Good Earth*. Schönberg startled Thalberg by announcing his terms, which included 'complete control' over the actors to ensure that they would 'speak in the same pitch and key' as his score, producing an effect, he promised, 'similar to *Pierrot Lunaire*, but, of course, less difficult'. Thalberg, in a cool hour some time later, let Schönberg know that he had come across some Chinese folk songs that had inspired the head of the music department to compose some 'lovely' music for the movie.[30] The studios, Eisler noted, were powerful enough to ignore the principled gesture. The composers who worked were generally the composers who were willing to adapt and conform. Composing for the movies had become little more than the routine selection of a standard musical device which would result in a specific audience effect already indicated in the dramatic scene. Composers became specialists in choosing the appropriate devices from the store-house of musical effects. A working knowledge of the popular classics thus formed the basis of the typical Hollywood composer's career. It was not unusual, for example, for relatively cheaply-made horror movies, such as *The Mummy* (1932), to be graced by music from such works as *Swan Lake*. As Max Winkler had confessed: 'We murdered the works of Mozart, Grieg, J.S. Bach, Verdi, Bizet, Tchaikovsky and Wagner – everything that wasn't protected by copyright from our pilfering.'[31]

Music had always been an important part of Adorno's life and work. Movies, on the other hand, were, at least during his stay in the U.S., impossible to ignore. Living near Los Angeles, during the early forties, he had a unique opportunity to witness the extraordinary impact of Hollywood movies. When he was preparing to begin work on his collaboration with Eisler, he sought out his old friend and fellow *émigré*, Siegfried Kracauer (who was working on his own major study of movies), for advice.[32] He was aware, after all, that he was far from being an expert on the subject. Unlike Eisler, he had not worked for the Hollywood studios, and his contact with other people involved in making movies was, it seems, relatively slight. He had much more experience, practical and theoretical, of making music. Indeed, his earliest work in America had involved the sociological analysis of radio music.

In New York, Adorno had worked half-time for the Institute and the other half for the Princeton Radio Research Project, directed by another *émigré*, Paul Lazarsfeld. Adorno's task was to direct the Music Study section of the Project. There were tensions from the very beginning. Lazarsfeld was a master of empirical social science techniques, which he encouraged Adorno to employ to test his theories about music and popular culture. Adorno was never convinced that such techniques were reliable and illuminating methods of understanding 'the utter obscurity of what we call "musical experience"':

> I hardly knew how to approach it. A small machine which enabled a listener to indicate what he liked and didn't like by pushing a button during the performance of a piece of music appeared to be highly inadequate to the complexity of what had to be discovered; and this in spite of the seeming objectivity of the data supplied. In any event, I was determined before I took the field to pursue in depth what could perhaps be called musical "content analysis", without confusing music with program music. I still recall how bewildered I was when my late colleague Franz Neumann ... asked me whether the questionnaires for the Music Study had already been sent out, when I still hardly knew whether the questions that I regarded as essential could be done justice to by questionnaires.[33]

Adorno continued to insist that culture is the condition 'that excludes a mentality capable of measuring it'.[34] He found a sympathetic colleague in George Simpson, an American sociologist who was also familiar with the European tradition. Simpson encouraged him to be as radical and uncompromising as he felt he needed to be, and assisted him in the writing of four articles based on his research. Adorno would later pay tribute to Simpson's invaluable support:

> Time and again I have observed that native Americans were more open-minded, above all more willing to help, than European immigrants. The latter, under the pressure of prejudice and rivalry, often showed the tendency to be more American than the Americans and were also quick to consider every newly arrived fellow European as a kind of threat to their own "adjustment".[35]

Although Adorno had begun, with Simpson's assistance, to transform his distinctive arguments into American sociological language, his role on the Project was terminated in 1940, when its sponsor, the Rockefeller Foundation, withdrew its support from the musical section.

Adorno's work within the Institute itself proved to be much more coherent and constructive. When he and Horkheimer moved to Santa Monica, they began work on a major (but by no means definitive) statement of their common position: *Dialectic of Enlightenment*.[36] One of their major concerns, and the one that was made to seem especially prominent because of their move near to Los Angeles, was the critique of mass culture. Mass culture, they insisted, had an important political function. It was a mass culture for a class society; far from arising spontaneously from the 'masses' themselves, as it presented itself as doing, it was actually imposed on them from above: 'The effrontery of the rhetorical question, "What do people want?" lies in the fact that it is addressed . . . to those very people who are deliberately to be deprived of this individuality.'[37] In order to distance themselves from the conventional idea of mass culture as a genuinely popular culture, Horkheimer and Adorno coined the polemical phrase 'the culture industry'. The expression was not meant to be taken entirely literally: it referred 'to the standardization of the thing itself – such as that of the Western, familiar to every movie-goer – and to the rationalization of distribution techniques, but not strictly to the production process'.[38]

The culture industry, they argued,

> perpetually cheats its consumers of what it perpetually promises. The promissory note which, with its plots and staging, it draws on pleasure is endlessly prolonged; the promise, which is actually all the spectacle consists of, is illusory: all it actually confirms is that the real point will never be reached, that the diner must be satisfied with the menu.[39]

The culture industry, integrated into capitalism, in turn integrates consumers from above. It operates to ensure its own reproduction; the cultural forms it produces must therefore be compatible with this aim. Cultural commodities must be instantly recognizable and attractive while seeming distinctive and new; the familiar must therefore be promoted as the unfamiliar, the old re-styled as the ever-new: routine standardization is thus obscured by 'pseudo-individualization':

Pseudo individuality is rife: from the standardized jazz improvisation to the exceptional film star whose hair curls over her eye to demonstrate her originality. What is individual is no more than the generality's power to stamp the accidental detail so firmly that it is accepted as such. The defiant reserve or elegant appearance of the individual on show is mass-produced like Yale locks, whose only difference can be measured in fractions of millimeters. The peculiarity of the self is a monopoly commodity determined by society; it is falsely represented as natural. It is no more than the moustache, the French accent, the deep voice of the woman of the world, the Lubitsch touch: finger prints on identity cards which are otherwise exactly the same.[40]

It is extremely important that one places this critique in its proper historical context. Adorno and Horkheimer were, as ever, seeking a 'theory for the times', a critical theory that concerned itself with timely, not timeless, interpretations and judgements of changing circumstances. Their Hollywood was the Hollywood of the late thirties and early forties, a Hollywood dominated by the immensely powerful studios. The movie industry was characterized by a small number of vertically-integrated companies: the so-called 'Big Five' studios – Warner Bros., RKO, 20th Century-Fox, Paramount and MGM – and the smaller Universal, Columbia and United Artists. The so-called 'studio system' was based on the oligopolistic control by the studios of production, distribution and exhibition. During the peak years of the studio system, the eight majors controlled 95 per cent of all movies exhibited in the U.S. As each of the major studios produced more movies every year, the centralization of administrative procedures became essential: buying stories, reserving stage space, controlling and co-ordinating the working schedules of performers, building sets and commissioning scores, were tasks assumed by managerial personnel who could oversee the entire complex operation. Production came to be organized increasingly on an 'assembly line' basis marked by highly-developed divisions of labour and hierarchies of authority and control. The screenwriters sometimes found themselves being spied on to check that they were always writing; actors were trained, groomed and sometimes re-styled. Stars, directors, writers, musicians and technicians were kept on contract by the studios. Each studio had its own repertory of leading men and women, character actors, singing stars and comedy acts. Each studio cultivated an instantly-recognizable style: Warner Bros, for example, tended to specialize in certain genres (gangster movies, backstage musicals and, later on, romantic adventures) with a distinctive 'look' (low-key lighting, simple sets) and a notably populist image, while Universal concentrated on expressionistic horror movies and MGM favoured large-budget costume dramas and lavish musicals.[41] It was this calculated appearance of diversity within a rationalized commercial system that Adorno and Horkheimer came to observe.

Hollywood was at that time, they felt, the real dream factory of the culture industry. Where there was once innovation, there was now imitation. Repetition had taken the place of development. The culture industry functioned like an enormous 'multiple-choice questionnaire' without a correct answer; what mattered now was not so much the choice itself but more the fact that one chose at all. The consequence, feared Horkheimer and Adorno, might eventually be a society without a sense of past or future, an individual without memory or imagination; history would be dissolved by the endless flow of the present. The spectre that was haunting this world was the 'spectre of man without memory',[42] without the ability to recall or dream that things could be other than they currently are. The culture industry encourages forgetfulness and distraction. The breathless pace of most Hollywood movies, for example, left little room for serious reflection on the part of the audience: 'The liberation which amusement promises is freedom from thought and from negation.'[43]

Adorno, earlier in his American exile, had noted the effects of this tendency on music; the familiarity of the musical work, he argued, 'is a surrogate for the quality ascribed to it. To like it is almost the same thing as to recognise it'.[44] Standardization sought standard responses. With the fetishism of music came the regression of hearing, a decline in the ability of the listener to concentrate on anything but the most truncated aspects of a composition. The process was by no means limited to the reception of so-called 'popular' music. Connoisseurs of 'serious' music were inclined to listen in the distracted manner promoted by classical programming: 'The tired businessman can clap arranged classics on the shoulder and fondle the progeny of their muse.'[45] 'Classical' works were either broken down into semi-precious gems ('the man who in the subway trium-phantly whistles loudly the theme of the finale of Brahms's First is already primarily involved in its debris'), or else were rescued from the clutches of exchange only to be fetishized for their quaint appearance of wholeness ('if the romanticizing of particulars eats away the body of the whole, the endangered substance is galvanically copper-plated').[46] Vulgarization and enchantment, the two 'hostile sisters, dwell together in the arrangements which have colonized large areas of music'.[47]

Adorno's specific criticisms of music in the movies were founded on his more general critique of the culture industry. He did not, as Eisler did, have direct experience of composing for the movies. Hollywood, he argued, was reducing music to the status of an advertisement for the very movie it appeared in. By lending the vision a veneer of humanity, music was obscuring the movie's absence of humanity. He compared the music which accompanied the movie's opening credits to a barker's spiel: 'Look here, everyone! What you will see is as grand, as radiant, as colourful as I am! Be grateful, clap your hands and buy.'[48]

By the 1940s, Adorno and Eisler were, in many ways, unlikely collaborators on a study of movie music. Theirs had been a troubled relationship from the very beginning, in 1925, when Alban Berg brought them together. Adorno was remarkably well-read, critically astute and intimidating, while Eisler was politically active and a celebrated young musician, and, it should be added, egregious modesty was certainly not one of either man's most remarked upon personal foibles. They regarded each other as potential rivals, although, it seems, they recognized and respected each other's talents. Adorno had written a very positive review of Eisler's Duo op. 7 for violin and cello, performed at the Venice Music Festival that same year. He described Eisler as 'the composer who represents Arnold Schönberg's latest generation of students', and praised the imaginative talent 'which may be very personal to him without being so overtly in evidence as his melodic inventiveness, his harmonic eloquence and his knowledge of his instruments'.[49] Eisler's controversial transitional work, *Zeitungsausschnitte* op. 11 for voice and piano, first performed in Berlin in December 1927, also attracted a sensitive and supportive response from Adorno, who commended the *brio* and distinctiveness of the songs. The two men had already begun to drift apart, however, at the same time that Eisler had rebelled against Schönberg.

Eisler attacked the 'new music' for what he regarded as its élitism; he believed. that it had 'turned a deaf ear' to the social conflicts of its times. As part of his practical protest against this perceived élitism, Eisler began his critique of musical culture immanently, through the text, renouncing bourgeois art while using bourgeois methods. The modern composer, declared Eisler, 'must change from a parasite into a fighter'. His own music was further transformed when, at the end of 1927, he joined the Berlin agit-prop group Das Rote Sprachrohr (The Red Mouthpiece) as its composer, pianist and conductor. In writing for the group, he learned how to express himself in a manner that, he felt, the working class could understand. A new kind of musical rhetoric was required, more basic and idiomatic, one that synthesized elements from accessible 'low' genres with the resources of modern music. Eisler composed a number of songs, incidental music and ballads for the group, including one of his most well-known, the *Kominternlied*.[50]

It was Eisler's insistent drive towards musical practice, uniting a sharp theoretical awareness with an urgent practical activity, that distinguished him from most other composers of his time. His project was, primarily, a political one: to give concrete musical expression to the Marxist vision of society and the aspirations of the working class. Eisler's militant songs and political ballads were to be distinguished by their topicality and precise political content, whose impact was heightened by the music. They were songs for the workers in the great modern cities, and they sought to lend their weight to the complex process of enlightening people about their own material interests.

This work had been encouraged by the vital figure of Brecht, who saw in Eisler a very appealing, and rare, combination of outstanding musical technique and urgent practical commitment. Their enduring collaborative relationship, which began in 1928, ranged from the didactic 'oratorio' *Die Massnahme* (1930) to the Schönbergian 'Hollywood Elegies' *Lieder* cycle (1942). To support Brecht's dramatic techniques Eisler developed compositional methods designed to break the audience's identification and immediate rapport with musical sonority so that music and text could, once again, be experienced consciously.

Adorno was opposed to this didactic form of art, which he regarded as akin to the reactionary 'community music' of composers such as Paul Hindemith. In stark contrast to Brecht and Eisler's self-consciously 'political' approach, Adorno argued that only a music that refuses easy communicability can be regarded as genuinely revolutionary. Music, he believed, was the index of the culture in which it was composed, all the more so because its codes are so hard to fathom. 'Works of art do not lie,' he said, 'what they say is literally true. Their reality, however, lies in the fact that they are answers to questions brought before them from outside.'[51] Radical music was music which recognized the disjunction that had occurred between art and social life, a disjunction which could not 'be corrected within music, but only within society'.[52] In modern art, he argued, 'direct protest is reactionary'.[53] According to Adorno, it was not constructive for music 'to stare in helpless horror at society'; music fulfilled its social function 'when it presents social problems through its own material and according to its own formal laws – problems which music contains within itself in the innermost cells of its technique'.[54] Genuinely autonomous art never settles, never rests, never allows itself to be taken in by its own designs: 'To be true to Schönberg', Adorno observed, 'is to warn against all twelve-tone schools.'[55]

Brecht's overtly political art, Adorno contended, only succeeded in making art apolitical. Although Adorno sympathized with Brecht's intentions (and the two men remained relatively friendly on a personal level), he was critical of his proposed solutions.[56] Far from making social reality appear strange, Brecht's dramatic techniques make it seem straightfoward – thus projecting yet another illusion which he underwrites by presenting it in such a coercive manner. His didactic posture, according to Adorno, 'reflects intolerance of ambiguity that touches off thought and reflection. In this Brecht is authoritarian ... [H]e wanted to be influential at all costs, if necessary by employing techniques of domination.'[57] Brecht, in turn, regarded Adorno and his Institute colleagues as politically complacent, having, in his view, defused their Marxism of its revolutionary urgency. Although he continued to socialize with them, he started to use them and their activities as raw material for his long-gestating, never-completed *Tui-Novel*, a satire on the follies of intellectuals that he had been working on since 1934. Eisler, himself stung by some of Adorno's criticisms, had encouraged Brecht to make such a critical connection; the latter recorded in his diary,

> With Eisler at Horkheimer's for lunch. After that, Eisler suggests for the Tui novel: the story of the Frankfurt Institute for Social Research. A wealthy old man dies, worried over the suffering in the world, leaves in his will a substantial sum of money establishing an institute that shall search for the source of misery – which of course was himself.[58]

(It is intriguing, not to say a little disturbing, to note that Brecht and Eisler could both miss the irony in making such a tart criticism after, presumably, they had both enjoyed a free lunch.) In a later remark, made from his East German home, Eisler would complain that 'half-baked' Marxists such as Adorno 'only want to be more clever than the bourgeois theorists, they do not want to take issue with them'.[59]

The episode remained a source of tension between the two camps. As late as 1978, Leo Löwenthal, as the last surviving critical theorist of that first generation, felt moved to offer a defence of the Institute: 'I have never heard that miserable living conditions and substandard nutrition are necessary prerequisites for innovative thought. If Marx and Nietzsche at times suffered insults of material deprivation, their theoretical creativity survived, not because of but despite such painful conditions.'[60] He also noted that this kind of critic sometimes 'found his own ways of comfortable survival' in the East, 'in a political environment where many other heretic Marxists', those not privy to the strategy of adaptive behaviour, 'had their heads chopped off'. As for Brecht's attack on Adorno and his colleagues for their 'failure' to unite theory with practice in an appropriately urgent manner, Löwenthal, with bitter sarcasm, replied:

> True, had Adorno and his friends manned the barricades, they might very well have been immortalized in a revolutionary song by Hanns Eisler. But imagine for a moment Marx dying on the barricades in 1849 or 1871: there would be no Marxism, no advanced psychological models, and certainly no Critical Theory.[61]

Adorno himself had responded to such criticisms on several occasions. 'Pseudo-activity', which congratulates itself on its radical gestures, measuring its engagement by the sweat of its brow, was, he argued, a reactionary phenomenon. The *genuinely* critical thinker, he insisted, was the one who was not afraid to speak the truth, even when the truth is difficult to come to terms with; the honestly committed theorist was the one 'who neither superscribes his conscience nor permits himself to be terrorized into action'.[62] Brecht's fetishized 'activism' was profoundly anti-Marxist, for it sought, through an act of will, to transcend the effects of capitalism's division of labour, a division of labour which a socialist revolution was supposed to destroy: 'The elitist segregation of the avant-garde', Adorno insisted, 'is not arts fault but society's.'[63] One should not confuse a depressing realism with an unjustified pessimism.

In their common exile in America, however, Eisler and Adorno were sufficiently motivated to collaborate in 1944 on a serious study of the composition and consumption of movie music. In 1939, Eisler, armed with a commission from Oxford University Press for a book on music in movies, won a grant of $20,000 from the Rockefeller Foundation for a research project on the subject. The object was to investigate the relationship between the movie, music, original sound and synthetic sound with a view to discovering new possibilities. The hypothesis was that radically new music could be much more constructive and effective in movies than the now cliché'd traditional music. The hypothesis was to be tested by a practical demonstration of how advanced musical material could be introduced into a movie score; four experimental productions were planned, with Eisler, using sequences from feature films and documentaries, contrasting the existing music with his own alternatives.

The heart of the project, and at the same time the starting point for the results that were later formulated in the book, was a detailed analysis of, and a subsequent composition for, an early silent film by Joris Ivens, *Rain* (1929). Numerous visual effects of rain had been filmed by Ivens as symbols of sorrow. Eisler composed music, in the form of variations for quintet, which he felt best captured the expressive possibilities of these images. The finished work, *Vierzehn Arten, den Regen zu beschreiben*, was regarded by Eisler as his most effective piece of chamber music.

The book that followed the project combined description with prescription, balancing Adorno's critique of standardized musical structures with Eisler's insistence on the possibility of overcoming them through the exposure of their mechanisms. The specific theoretical underpinnings of the book, particularly evident in its early critique of the culture industry, point clearly to Adorno's influence. Those moments in the text when the two authors seem to speak with one voice occur in the context of the analysis of the shortcomings of common commercial movie music. The first two chapters, in particular, on 'Prejudices and Bad Habits' and 'Function and Dramaturgy', and the fourth, on 'Sociological Aspects', carry the inner cadence of Adorno's distinctive critique of the culture industry. Movies, it is argued, cannot be understood in isolation, but only as 'the most characteristic medium' of the culture industry.[64] The standardized Hollywood movie of the period was marked by the 'pretense to immediacy', a pretence which masked the contradictions inherent in the medium (such as its technological nature and its administrative remoteness). Movie music served to underscore the movie's illusion of immediate, naked life, bringing 'the picture close to the public, just as the picture brings itself close to it by means of the close-up'; the music works to 'interpose a human coating between the reeled-off pictures and the spectators'.[65] Ultimately, the methods and results discourage real contact in production or consumption between a movie and the actual needs of its consumers.

The character of movie music was determined by the immediate needs of the industry. The music had no autonomy: in subordinating itself to a text outside itself, it offered the opposite of Adorno's aesthetic standard of generating musical meaning. All the music 'is under the sign of utility', to be 'tolerated as an outsider who is somehow regarded as being indispensable' (partly because of a practical need and partly because of the fetishistic idea that all the existing technical resources should be exploited to the full).[66] Far from representing a contradiction of the silent movie, the synchronized sound movie is its continuation; music remains on the side of the image, the apparently artificial musical score being a psychological condition for the existence of the apparently natural movie image. A number of standard practices are singled out by the authors for criticism: the leitmotif, whose 'classical' function had 'been reduced to the level of a musical lackey, who announces his master with an important air even though the eminent passage is clearly recognizable to everyone';[67] melody and euphony, employed for their immediate 'easy intelligibility'; unobtrusiveness, 'the premise that the spectator should not be conscious of the music';[68] visual justification, whereby music, out of a chronic fear of silence in an age of sound, becomes 'a sort of acoustical stage property', as in the musical imitation of a storm;[69] illustration, whereby music mimics visual incidents either through slavish imitation or the use of basic melodic clichés for moods; geography and history, in which music, like costume, 'cues' the spectator to the setting; stock music, which transforms, for example, the *Moonlight Sonata* into a mere signpost, a sound trademark, to accompany stock dramatic events; *clichés*, standardized details which contribute to the 'elaboration of typical situations'; and standardized interpretation, the form of pseudo-individualization which, as Adorno wrote elsewhere, 'fools us about predigestion'.[70]

In a passage which echoes Adorno's earlier essay on the fetishism of music and the concomitant regression of hearing, the authors stress the 'archaic' character of acoustical perception, its ability to preserve 'traits of long bygone, pre-individualistic collectivities' more effectively than optical perception, and the regressive process whereby industrial capitalism debases the nature of hearing through commercialized music, mechanical mass-reproduction, and the utilization of music in advertising. The communal, hedonistic, utopian elements of musical perception had been fetishized, 'put into the service of commercialism'. Music, the memory – and anticipation – of collectivities, had become the 'medium in which irrationality can be practiced rationally'.[71] The commercial movie score encouraged identification: emotional proximity was achieved by means of a familiar musical language and an identity of sound and vision which screened out contradictions and projected an impression of wholeness with which the spectator could identify. This was the problem, stated by the authors as provocatively as possible. There was, however, a possible solution.

Movie audiences, in spite of the effects of the culture industry, had not yet become completely passive: 'resistance and spontaneity still survive'.[72] Eisler's distinctive perspective becomes more discernible here, as a critical strategy is sketched out. Although Adorno agreed with Eisler's conviction that there still existed the potential for critical reflection and action, he was sceptical of Eisler's specific practical proposals. Drawing on his own experience of composing music for Hollywood movies, such as *Hangmen Also Die*,[73] Eisler insisted that the 'task is not to compose ordinary music for unusual instruments', but, on the contrary, 'it is more important to compose unusual music for ordinary instruments'.[74] The composer, he argued, needed the power to exert greater influence, as consultant on and contributor to the movie-making process, entering the production at the beginning, rather than the end, and working with, rather than for, the screenwriters and director. Movie music should speak with its own voice; it should act as well as react. The use of music in the movie really should be inspired by 'the intrinsic requirements of the work'.[75] Each movie must establish its own unique relations. A 'proper' dramaturgy would distinguish sharply between 'pictures, words, and music, and for that very reason [would] relate them meaningfully to one another'. The proper aim of the composer should be 'to compose music that, even if it is listened to inattentively, can as a whole be perceived correctly and adequately to its function, without having to move along beaten associative tracks that help the listener to grasp the music, but block any adequate fulfilment of its function'. The familiar should be made unfamiliar, the normal made strange, encouraging a more troubled kind of entertainment. Good cinema music 'should sparkle and glisten', working to 'make everything completely sensuous', achieving whatever it achieves 'on the surface' rather than becoming 'lost in itself'.[76]

Composing for the Films is, in many ways, an uncomfortable and sometimes frustrating hybrid of a book, reflecting (as well as, at times, threatening to transcend) the distinct dispositions and styles of the two co-authors. Some of the more deliberately provocative and felicitous comparisons (such as the remark that the musical accompaniment to the images 'converts a kiss into a magazine cover, an outburst of unmitigated pain into a melodrama, a scene from nature into an oleograph'[77]) would not have been out of place in Adorno and Horkheimer's knowingly elliptical *Dialectic of Enlightenment*. The Adornian juxtapositions and exaggerations, however, can perhaps best be seen to work constructively to open up a space for Eisler's critical imagination, alerting one simultaneously to the seriousness of the current problems and the urgency of the proposed solutions. As the two authors noted:

> In order to emphasize the "critical" ideas by means of which the existing stagnation can be overcome, drastic examples have been chosen, extreme instances that do not, however, preclude the possibility of a less pointed relationship between modern pictures and music.[78]

The text is at its least coherent, however, at those places late on in the discussion where Adorno's theoretical argument is obscured and, apparently, contradicted by Eisler's more pragmatic approach. Eisler's evident confidence came, in part, from the memory of the best moments in his own Hollywood experiences working with sympathetic writers and directors, such as Brecht, Odets, Sirk and Renoir. It is not very clear, none the less, how Eisler would have been able to compose a successful and suitable score, one that had a genuinely emancipatory effect on the movie in which it was set, without alienating either, or both, the producers or the consumers – both of whom were, it seemed, steeped thoroughly in the identification he wished to undermine. At the end of the discussion, it has to be said, Adorno's criticisms remain rather more convincing than Eisler's prescriptions.

If *Composing for the Films* had a peculiar conception, it also had a difficult birth. It first appeared in English, published in New York by Oxford University Press in 1947 (and in London by Dennis Dobson in 1951), under Eisler's name alone. In his preface Eisler acknowledged that the 'theories and formulations presented here evolved from co-operation with [Adorno] on general aesthetic and sociological matters as well as purely musical issues'. According to some sources, Adorno withdrew his name as co-author in order to avoid being implicated in the House Un-American Activities Committee's investigations into Eisler's political associations (his brother, Gerhart, was a well-known communist who had been interrogated by the Committee early in 1947).[79] It was certainly true that Eisler was regarded by the Committee as a very suspicious figure. Although he, like Brecht, had never actually been a member of the Communist Party, he had never tried to disguise his politicial beliefs. Eisler's sister, Ruth Fischer, who had lived in the U.S. since 1941, denounced him and Gerhart to the FBI, and wrote a number of fiercely critical articles against them which made the front page of several leading American newspapers. Fischer, since her expulsion from the German Communist Party in 1926, was a bitter figure for whom the new anti-communist movement proved highly opportune. She now sought to drive her two brothers, among others, out of the country. 'In your family', Charlie Chaplin remarked to the demoralized Eisler, 'things happen as in Shakespeare.'[80]

In April 1947, Richard Nixon, a Californian delegate of one year, declared that the Committee was about to begin collecting 'facts' concerning Eisler's activities and political affiliations: 'The case of Hanns Eisler', he said, ominously, 'is perhaps the most important ever to have come before the Committee.'[81] Eisler was first interrogated in Hollywood in May, followed by a three-day interrogation in Washington in September. Robert Stripling, the chief interrogator, informed the chairman of the Committee, Parnell Thomas, that his purpose was 'to show that Mr Eisler is the Karl Marx of communism in the musical field and he is well aware of it'.[82] Eisler replied that he 'would be flattered' by such a comparison. His case was a very significant one; a committee was founded for his defence, and he received considerable public support from other luminaries, such as Picasso, Chaplin, Matisse, Cocteau, Einstein and Thomas Mann. It was to no avail; he judged it advisable to leave the country early in 1948.

Eisler, in his remaining years, did not revise his basic ideas on movies and their use of music in any fundamental way; indeed, in his testimony to the House Committee on Un-American Activities he had gone on record as claiming *Composing for the Films* as his artistic credo. Adorno, however, while continuing his critique of the culture industry, did, during the sixties, devote more space to the discussion of the critical potential that was still inherent in certain aspects of modern art.[83]

A slightly revised edition of the book, *Komposition für den Film*, without any credit accorded to Adorno, was published in Berlin in 1949 by Bruno Henschel und Sohn. It was only when the original version, authorized by Adorno, was translated and reprinted in West Germany in 1969 by Rogner & Bernhard that Adorno was finally acknowledged on the cover as co-author.[84] The book became a curious kind of classic: a study which marked the results of a pioneering analysis of the character and potential of film music; a rare collaboration which represented a unique attempt at finding some common ground between Brechtian practice and Critical Theory; and a book which was often cited but seldom read.

It deserves to be rediscovered today. It makes musicians take note of politics, and political theorists take note of music; the signature it signs is memorably unorthodox. Many of its arguments continue to command respect. Hollywood still appears to favour the idea that music in movies should be easy on the ear and should know its place. The commercial soundtrack, for example, marketed in record form, suggests that the culture industry persists in celebrating, and benefiting from, its integrative powers. The original demand for a radical change in practice continues to go unanswered. The promissory note, however, goes on being played; hope can still, faintly, be heard. Adorno once likened his theoretical efforts to 'messages in bottles on the flood of barbarism'.[85] *Composing for the Films* can be seen as one such message, still afloat, and still in search of its unknown addressee.

Editor's Note
Footnotes in the text added by the editor for this edition have been incorporated with the original notes.

The index has been compiled for this Continuum edition.

Preface

This small book, an account of theoretical and practical experiences with cinema music, is an outcome of the Film Music Project of the New School for Social Research, financed by the Rockefeller Foundation. When I took charge of the direction of this Project, it was at once foreseen that the results would have to be published. The several years I spent in Hollywood made it possible for me to expand the book by considering the problems of music within the practical set-up of the motion-picture industry. However, I neither aimed at systematic completion nor ever intended to make a survey of contemporary motion-picture music and its tendencies. The guiding point of view was that of the composer who tries to become conscious of the requirements, conditions, and intrinsic obstacles of his work.

The Film Music Project is indebted to Alvin Johnson, President Emeritus of the New School; its dean, Clara Mayer; and John Marshall of the Rockefeller Foundation, without whose active co-operation this study never would have come into being.

With regard to the present book, my thanks go, above all, to T. W. Adorno, who conducted the music division of another Rockefeller undertaking, the Princeton Radio Research Project. The problems with which he had to concern himself were those of a social, musical, and even technical aspect, closely related to the moving picture. The theories and formulations presented here evolved from co-operation with him on general aesthetic and sociological matters as well as purely musical issues.

I wish to mention the names of Clifford Odets, Jean Renoir, and Harold Clurman, contact with whom was very important. Reference should also be made to the poet Bertolt Brecht, who stresses throughout his work the gestural elements of music.

The art of Charles Chaplin proved to be a continuous inspiration.

Finally I wish to express my thanks to George MacManus and Norbert Guterman for their help in the translation and editing of the manuscript. The publishers Harcourt, Brace and Company and Faber and Faber have kindly permitted the use of quotations and musical examples from *The Film Sense* by Serge Eisenstein and *Film Music* by Kurt London.

Hanns Eisler
Los Angeles, California

Introduction

The motion picture cannot be understood in isolation, as a specific form of art; it is understandable only as the most characteristic medium of contemporary cultural industry, which uses the techniques of mechanical reproduction. The popular messages conveyed by this industry must not be conceived as an art originally created by the masses. Such an art no longer exists or does not yet exist. Even the vestiges of spontaneous folk art have died out in the industrialized countries; at best it subsists in backward agrarian regions. In this advanced industrial age, the masses are compelled to seek relaxation and rest, in order to restore the labor power that has been spent in the alienated process of labor; and this need is the mass basis of mass culture. On it there has arisen the powerful amusement industry, which constantly produces, satisfies, and reproduces new needs.

   Cultural industry is not a product of the twentieth century; however, it is only in the course of the last decades that it has been monopolized and thoroughly organized. And because of this process, it has assumed an entirely new character – it has become inescapable. Taste and receptivity have become largely standardized; and, despite the multiplicity of products, the consumer has only apparent freedom of choice. Production has been divided into administrative fields, and whatever passes through the machinery bears its mark, is predigested, neutralized, levelled down. The old distinction between serious and popular art, between low-grade and refined autonomous art, no longer applies. All art, as a means of filling out leisure time, has become entertainment, although it absorbs materials and forms of traditional autonomous art as part of the so-called 'cultural heritage.' It is this very process of amalgamation that abolishes aesthetic autonomy: what happens to the *Moonlight Sonata* when it is sung by a choir and played by a supposedly mystical orchestra now actually happens to everything. Art that does not yield is completely shut off from consumption and driven into isolation. Everything is taken apart, robbed of its real meaning, and then put together again. The only criterion of this procedure is that of reaching the consumer as effectively as possible. Manipulated art is consumer's art.

Of all the media of cultural industry, the motion picture, as the most comprehensive, most clearly displays this tendency to amalgamation. The development and integration of its technical elements – pictures, words, sound, script, acting, and photography – have paralleled certain social tendencies to amalgamation of traditional cultural values that have become commodities. Such tendencies were operative earlier – in Wagner's music dramas; in Reinhardt's neo-romantic theater, and in the symphonic poems of Liszt and Strauss; later they were consummated in the motion picture as the amalgamation of drama, psychological novel, dime novel, operetta, symphony concert, and revue.

Critical insight into the nature of industrialized culture does not imply sentimental glorification of the past. It is no accident that this culture thrives parasitically on the products of the old individualistic age. The old individualistic mode of production should not be set up against it as necessarily superior to it, nor should technology as such be held responsible for the barbarism of the cultural industry. On the other hand, the technical advances, which are the triumphs of the cultural industry, must not be accepted under all circumstances. Which technical resources should be used in art should be determined by intrinsic requirements. Technology opens up unlimited opportunities for art in the future, and even in the poorest motion pictures there are moments when such opportunities are strikingly apparent. But the same principle that has opened up these opportunities also ties them to big business. A discussion of industrialized culture must show the interaction of these two factors: the aesthetic potentialities of mass art in the future, and its ideological character at present.

The following pages are intended as a partial contribution to this task. In them we have dealt with a strictly delimited segment of the cultural industry, namely the technical and social potentialities and contradictions of music in relation to motion pictures.

1
Prejudices and Bad Habits

The character of motion-picture music has been determined by everyday practice. It has been an adaptation in part to the immediate needs of the film industry, in part to whatever musical clichés and ideas about music happened to be current. As a result, a number of empirical standards – rules of thumb – were evolved that corresponded to what motion-picture people called common sense. These rules have now been made obsolete by the technical development of the cinema as well as of autonomous music, yet they have persisted as tenaciously as if they had their roots in ancient wisdom rather than in bad habits. They originated in the intellectual milieu of Tin Pan Alley; and because of practical considerations and problems of personnel, they have so entrenched themselves that they, more than anything else, have hindered the progress of motion-picture music. They only seem to make sense as a consequence of standardization within the industry itself, which calls for standard practices everywhere.

Furthermore, these rules of thumb represent a kind of pseudo-tradition harking back to the days of spontaneity and craftsmanship, of medicine shows and covered wagons. And it is precisely this discrepancy between obsolete practices and scientific production methods that characterizes the whole system. The two aspects are inseparable in principle, and both are subject to criticism. Public realization of the antiquated character of these rules should suffice to break their hold.

Typical examples of these habits, selected at random, will be discussed here in order to show concretely the level on which the problem of motion-picture music is dealt with today.

The Leitmotif

Cinema music is still patched together by means of leitmotifs. The ease with which they are recalled provides definite clues for the listener, and they also are a practical help to the composer in his task of composition under pressure. He can quote where he otherwise would have to invent.

The idea of the leitmotif has been popular since the days of Wagner.[1] His popularity was largely connected with his use of leitmotifs. They function as trademarks, so to speak, by which persons, emotions, and symbols can instantly be identified. They have always been the most elementary means of elucidation, the thread by which the musically inexperienced find their way about. They were drummed into the listener's ear by persistent repetition, often with scarcely any variation, very much as a new song is plugged or as a motion-picture actress is popularized by her hair-do. It was natural to assume that this device, because it is so easy to grasp, would be particularly suitable to motion pictures, which are based on the premise that they must be easily understood. However, the truth of this assumption is only illusory.

The reasons for this are first of all technical. The fundamental character of the leitmotif – its salience and brevity – was related to the gigantic dimensions of the Wagnerian and post-Wagnerian music dramas. Just because the leitmotif as such is musically rudimentary, it requires a large musical canvas if it is to take on a structural meaning beyond that of a signpost. The atomization of the musical element is paralleled by the heroic dimensions of the composition as a whole. This relation is entirely absent in the motion picture, which requires continual interruption of one element by another rather than continuity. The constantly changing scenes are characteristic of the structure of the motion picture. Musically, also, shorter forms prevail, and the leitmotif is unsuitable here because of this brevity of forms which must be complete in themselves. Cinema music is so easily understood that it has no need of leitmotifs to serve as signposts, and its limited dimension does not permit of adequate expansion of the leitmotif.

Similar considerations apply with regard to the aesthetic problem. The Wagnerian leitmotif is inseparably connected with the symbolic nature of the music drama. The leitmotif is not supposed merely to characterize persons, emotions, or things, although this is the prevalent conception. Wagner conceived its purpose as the endowment of the dramatic events with metaphysical significance. When in the *Ring* the tubas blare the

Valhalla motif, it is not merely to indicate the dwelling place of Wotan. Wagner meant also to connote the sphere of sublimity, the cosmic will, and the primal principle. The leitmotif was invented essentially for this kind of symbolism. There is no place for it in the motion picture, which seeks to depict reality. Here the function of the leitmotif has been reduced to the level of a musical lackey, who announces his master with an important air even though the eminent personage is clearly recognizable to everyone. The effective technique of the past thus becomes a mere duplication, ineffective and uneconomical. At the same time, since it cannot be developed to its full musical significance in the motion picture, its use leads to extreme poverty of composition.

Melody and Euphony

The demand for melody and euphony is not only assumed to be obvious, but also a matter of public taste, as represented in the consumer. We do not deny that producers and consumers generally agree in regard to this demand. But the concepts of melody and euphony are not so self-evident as is generally believed. Both are to a large extent conventionalized historical categories.

The concept of melody first gained ascendancy in the nineteenth century in connection with the new *Kunstlied,* especially Schubert's. Melody was conceived as the opposite of the 'theme' of the Viennese classicism of Haydn, Mozart, and Beethoven.[2] It denotes a tonal sequence, constituting not so much the point of departure of a composition as a self-contained entity that is easy to listen to, singable, and expressive. This notion led to the sort of melodiousness for which the German language has no specific term, but which the English word 'tune' expresses quite accurately. It consists first of all in the uninterrupted flow of a melody in the upper voice, in such a way that the melodic continuity seems natural, because it is almost possible to guess in advance exactly what will follow. The listener zealously insists on his right to this anticipation, and feels cheated if it is denied him. This fetishism in regard to melody, which at certain moments during the latter part of the Romantic period crowded out all the other elements of music, shackled the concept of melody itself.

Today, the conventional concept of melody is based on criteria of the crudest sort. Easy intelligibility is guaranteed by harmonic and rhythmic symmetry, and by the paraphrasing of accepted harmonic procedures;

tunefulness is assured by the preponderance of small diatonic intervals. These postulates have taken on the semblance of logic, owing to the rigid institutionalization of prevailing customs, in which these criteria automatically obtain. In Mozart's and Beethoven's day, when the stylistic ideal of filigree composition held sway, the postulate of the predominance of an anticipatable melody in the upper voice would scarcely have been comprehended. 'Natural' melody is a figment of the imagination, an extremely relative phenomenon illegitimately absolutized, neither an obligatory nor an *a priori* constituent of the material, but one procedure among many, singled out for exclusive use.

The conventional demand for melody and euphony is constantly in conflict with the objective requirements of the motion picture. The prerequisite of melody is that the composer be independent, in the sense that his selection and invention relate to situations that supply specific lyric-poetic inspiration. This is out of the question where the motion picture is concerned. All music in the motion picture is under the sign of utility, rather than lyric expressiveness. Aside from the fact that lyric-poetic inspiration cannot be expected of the composer for the cinema, this kind of inspiration would contradict the embellishing and subordinate function that industrial practice still enforces on the composer.

Moreover, the problem of melody as 'poetic' is made insoluble by the conventionality of the popular notion of melody. Visual action in the motion picture has of course a prosaic irregularity and asymmetry. It claims to be photographed life; and as such every motion picture is a documentary. As a result, there is a gap between what is happening on the screen and the symmetrically articulated conventional melody. A photographed kiss cannot actually be synchronized with an eight-bar phrase. The disparity between symmetry and asymmetry becomes particularly striking when music is used to accompany natural phenomena, such as drifting clouds, sunrises, wind, and rain. These natural phenomena could inspire nineteenth-century poets; however, as photographed, they are essentially irregular and nonrhythmic, thus excluding that element of poetic rhythm with which the motion-picture industry associates them. Verlaine could write a poem about rain in the city, but one cannot hum a tune that accompanies rain reproduced on the screen.

More than anything else the demand for melody at any cost and on every occasion has throttled the development of motion-picture music. The alternative is certainly not to resort to the unmelodic, but to liberate melody from conventional fetters.

Unobtrusiveness

One of the most widespread prejudices in the motion-picture industry is the premise that the spectator should not be conscious of the music. The philosophy behind this belief is a vague notion that music should have a subordinate role in relation to the picture. As a rule, the motion picture represents action with dialogue. Financial considerations and technical interest are concentrated on the actor; anything that might overshadow him is considered disturbing. The musical indications in the scripts are usually sporadic and indefinite. Music thus far has not been treated in accordance with its specific potentialities. It is tolerated as an outsider who is somehow regarded as being indispensable, partly because of a genuine need and partly on account of the fetishistic idea that the existing technical resources must be exploited to the fullest extent.[3]

Despite the often reiterated opinion of the wizards of the movie industry, in which many composers concur, the thesis that music should be unobtrusive is questionable. There are, doubtless, situations in motion pictures in which the dialogue must be emphasized and in which detailed musical foreground configurations would be disturbing. It may also be granted that these situations sometimes require acoustic supplementation. But precisely when this requirement is taken seriously, the insertion of allegedly unobtrusive music becomes dubious. In such instances, an accompaniment of extra-musical sound would more nearly approximate the realism of the motion picture. If, instead, music is used, music that is supposed to be real music but is not supposed to be noticed, the effect is that described in a German nursery rhyme:

> Ich weiss ein schönes Spiel,
> Ich mal' mir einen Bart,
> Und halt mir einen Fächer vor,
> Dass niemand ihn gewahrt.

> [I know a pretty game:
> I deck me with a beard
> And hide behind a fan
> So I won't look too weird.]*

In practice, the requirement of unobtrusiveness is generally met not by an approximation of nonmusical sounds, but by the use of banal music.

Accordingly, the music is supposed to be inconspicuous in the same sense as are selections from *La Bohème* played in a restaurant.

Apart from this, unobtrusive music, assumed to be the typical solution of the problem, is only one and certainly the least important of many possible solutions. The insertion of music should be planned along with the writing of the script, and the question whether the spectator should be aware of the music is a matter to be decided in each case according to the dramatic requirements of the script. Interruption of the action by a developed musical episode could be an important artistic device. For example, in an anti-Nazi picture, at the point when the action is dispersed into individual psychological details, an exceptionally serious piece of music occupies the whole perception. Its movement helps the listener to remember the essential incidents and focuses his attention on the situation as a whole. It is true that in this case the music is the very opposite of what it is conventionally supposed to be. It no longer expresses the conflicts of individual characters, nor does it persuade the spectator to identify himself with the hero; but rather it leads him back from the sphere of privacy to the major social issue. In pictures of an inferior type of entertainment – musicals and revues from which every trace of dramatic psychology is eliminated – one finds, more often than elsewhere, rudiments of this device of musical interruption, and the independent use of music in songs, dances, and finales.

Visual Justification

The problem relates less to rules than to tendencies, which are not as important as they were a few years ago, yet must still be taken into account. The fear that the use of music at a point when it would be completely impossible in a real situation will appear naive or childish, or impose upon the listener an effort of imagination that might distract him from the main issue, leads to attempts to justify this use in a more or less rationalistic way. Thus situations are often contrived in which it is allegedly natural for the main character to stop and sing, or music accompanying a love scene is made plausible by having the hero turn on a radio or a phonograph.

The following is a typical instance. The hero is waiting for his beloved. Not a word is spoken. The director feels the need of filling in the silence. He knows the danger of nonaction, of absence of suspense, and therefore prescribes music. At the same time, however, he lays so much stress in the objective portrayal of psychological continuity that an unmotivated irruption of music strikes him as risky. Thus he resorts to the most artless trick in order to avoid artlessness, and makes the hero turn to the radio. The threadbareness of this artifice is illustrated by those scenes in which the hero accompanies himself 'realistically' on the piano for about eight bars, whereupon he is relieved by a large orchestra and chorus, albeit with no change of scene. In so far as this device, which obtained in the early days of sound pictures, is still applied, it hinders the use of music as a genuine element of contrast. Music becomes a plot accessory, a sort of acoustical stage property.

Illustration

There is a favourite Hollywood gibe: 'Birdie sings, music sings.' Music must follow visual incidents and illustrate them either by directly imitating them or by using clichés that are associated with the mood and content of the picture. The preferred material for imitation is 'nature,' in the most superficial sense of the word, i.e. as the antithesis of the urban – that realm where people are supposed to be able to breathe freely, stimulated by the presence of plants and animals. This is a vulgar and stereotyped version of the concept of nature that prevailed in nineteenth-century poetry. Music is concocted to go with meretricious lyrics. Particularly landscape shots without action seem to call for musical accompaniment, which then conforms to the stale programmatic patterns. Mountain peaks invariably invoke string tremolos punctuated by a signal-like horn motif. The ranch to which the virile hero has eloped with the sophisticated heroine is accompanied by forest murmurs and a flute melody. A slow waltz goes along with a moonlit scene in which a boat drifts down a river lined with weeping willows.

What is in question here is not the principle of musical illustration. certainly musical illustration is only one among many dramaturgic resources, but it is so overworked that it deserves a rest, or at least it should be used with the greatest discrimination. This is what is generally lacking in prevailing practice. Music cut to fit the stereotype 'nature' is reduced to the character of a cheap mood-producing gadget, and the associative patterns are so familiar that there is really no illustration of anything, but only the elicitation of the automatic response: 'Aha, nature!'

Illustrative use of music today results in unfortunate duplication. It is uneconomical, except where quite specific effects are intended, or minute interpretation of the action of the picture. The old operas left a certain amount of elbow room in their scenic arrangements for what is vague and indefinite; this could be filled out with tone painting. The music of the Wagnerian era was actually a means of elucidation. But in the cinema, both picture and dialogue are hyperexplicit. Conventional music can add nothing to the explicitness, but instead may detract from it, since even in the worst pictures standardized musical effects fail to keep up with the concrete elaboration of the screen action. But if the elucidating function is given up as superfluous, music should never attempt to accompany precise occurrences in an imprecise manner. It should stick to its task even if it is only as questionable a one as that of creating a mood – renouncing that of repeating the obvious. Musical illustration should either be hyperexplicit itself – over-illuminating, so to speak, and thereby interpretive – or should be omitted. There is no excuse for flute melodies that force a bird call into a pattern of full ninth chords.

Geography and History

When the scene is laid in a Dutch town, with its canals, windmills, and wooden shoes, the composer is supposed to send over to the studio library for a Dutch folk song in order to use its theme as a working basis. Since it is not easy to recognize a Dutch folk song for what it is, especially when it has been subjected to the whims of an arranger, this procedure seems a dubious one. Here music is used in much the same way as costumes or sets, but without as strong a characterizing effect. A composer can attain something more convincing by writing a tune of his own on the basis of a village dance for little Dutch girls than he can by clinging to the original. Indeed, the current folk music of all countries – apart from that which is basically outside occidental music – tends toward a certain sameness, in contrast to the differentiated art languages. This is because it is grounded on a limited number of elementary rhythmic formulas associated with festivities, communal dances, and the like. It is as difficult to distinguish between the temperamental characters of Polish and Spanish dances, particularly in the conventionalized form they assumed in the nineteenth century, as it is to discern the difference between hill-billy songs and Upper Bavarian *Schnaderhüpferln*. Moreover, ordinary cinematic music has an irresistible urge to follow the pattern of 'just folk music.' Specific national characteristics can be captured musically only if the musical counterpart of beflagging the scene with national emblems like an exhibition is not resorted to. Related to this is the practice of investing costume pictures with music of the corresponding historical period. This recalls concerts in which hoop-skirted elderly ladies play tedious pre-Bach harpsichord pieces by candlelight in baroque palaces. The absurdity of such 'applied art' arrangements is glaring in contrast with the technique of the film, which is of necessity modern. If costume pictures must be, they might be better served by the free use of advanced musical resources.

Stock Music

One of the worst practices is the incessant use of a limited number of worn-out musical pieces that are associated with the given screen situations by reason of their actual or traditional titles. Thus, the scene of a moonlit night is accompanied by the first movement of the *Moonlight Sonata,* orchestrated in a manner that completely contradicts its meaning, because the piano melody – suggested by Beethoven with the utmost discretion – is made obtrusive and is richly underscored by the strings. For thunderstorms, the overture to *William Tell* is used; for weddings, the march from *Lohengrin* or Mendelssohn's wedding march. These practices – incidentally, they are on the wane and are retained only in cheap pictures – correspond to the popularity of trademarked pieces in classical music, such as Beethoven's E-flat Concerto, which has attained an almost fatal popularity under the apocryphal title *The Emperor,* or Schubert's *Unfinished Symphony.* The present vogue of the latter is to some extent connected with the idea that the composer died before it was finished, whereas he simply laid it aside years before his death. The use of trademarks is a nuisance, though it must be acknowledged that childlike faith in the eternal symbolic force of certain classical wedding or funeral marches occasionally has a redeeming aspect, when these are compared with original scores manufactured to order.

Clichés

All these questions are related to a more general state of affairs. Mass production of motion pictures has led to the elaboration of typical situations, ever-recurring emotional crises, and standardized methods of arousing suspense. They correspond to cliché effects in music. But music is often brought into play at the very point where particularly characteristic effects are sought for the sake of 'atmosphere' or suspense. The powerful effect intended does not come off, because the listener has been made familiar with the stimulus by innumerable analogous passages. Psychologically, the whole phenomenon is ambiguous. If the screen shows a peaceful country house while the music produces familiar sinister sounds, the spectator knows at once that something terrible is about to happen, and thus the musical accompaniment both intensifies the suspense and nullifies it by betraying the sequel.

As in many other aspects of contemporary motion pictures, it is not standardization as such that is objectionable here. Pictures that frankly follow an established pattern, such as 'westerns' or gangster and horror pictures, often are in a certain way superior to pretentious grade-A films. What is objectionable is the standardized character of pictures that claim to be unique; or, conversely, the individual disguise of the standardized pattern. This is exactly what happens in music. Thus, for example, throbbing and torrential string arpeggios – which the guides to Wagner once called the 'agitated motif' – are resorted to without rhyme or reason, and nothing can be more laughable to anyone who recognizes them for what they are.

Such musical conventions are all the more dubious because their material is usually taken from the most recently bygone phase of autonomous music, which still passes as 'modern' in motion pictures. Forty years ago, when musical impressionism and exoticism were at their height, the whole-tone scale was regarded as a particularly stimulating, unfamiliar, and 'colorful' musical device. Today the whole-tone scale is stuffed into the introduction of every popular hit, yet in motion pictures it continues to be used as if it had just seen the light of day. Thus the means employed and the *effect* achieved are completely disproportionate. Such a disproportion can have a certain charm when, as in animated cartoons, it serves to stress the absurdity of something impossible, for instance, Pluto galloping over the ice to the ride of the Walkyries. But the whole-tone scale so overworked in the amusement industry can no longer cause anyone really to shudder.

The use of clichés also affects instrumentation. The tremolo on the bridge of the violin, which thirty years ago was intended even in serious music to produce a feeling of uncanny suspense and to express an unreal atmosphere, today has become common currency. Generally, all artistic means that were originally conceived for their stimulating effect rather than for their structural significance grow threadbare and obsolete with extraordinary rapidity. Here, as in many other instances, the motion-picture industry is carrying out a sentence long since pronounced in serious music, and one is justified in ascribing a progressive function to the sound film in so far as it thus has discredited the trashy devices intended merely for effect. These have long since become unbearable both to artists and to the audience, so much so that sooner or later no one will be able to enjoy clichés. When this happens there will be both need and room for other elements of music. The development of *avant-garde* music in the course of the last thirty years has opened up an inexhaustible reservoir of new resources and possibilities that is still practically untouched. There is no objective reason why motion-picture music should not draw upon it.

Standardized Interpretation

The standardization of motion-picture music is particularly apparent in the prevailing style of performance. First of all, there is the element of dynamics, which was at one time limited by the imperfection of the recording and reproduction machinery. Today, this machinery is far better differentiated and affords far greater dynamic possibilities, both as regards the extremes and the transitions; nevertheless, standardization of dynamics still persists. The different degrees of strength are levelled and blurred to a general mezzoforte – incidentally, this practice is quite analogous to the habits of the mixer in radio broadcasting. The main purpose here is the production of a comfortable and polished euphony, which neither startles by its power (fortissimo) nor requires attentive listening because of its weakness (pianissimo). In consequence of this levelling, dynamics as a means of elucidating musical contexts is lost. The lack of a threefold fortissimo and pianissimo reduces the crescendo and decrescendo to too small a range.

In the methods of performance, too, standardization has as its counterpart pseudo-individualization.[4] While everything is more or less adjusted to the mezzoforte ideal, an effort is made, through exaggerated interpretation, to make each musical motif produce the utmost expression, emotion, and suspense. The violins must sob or scintillate, the brasses must crash insolently or bombastically, no moderate expression is tolerated, and the whole method of performance is based on exaggeration. It is characterized by a mania for extremes, such as were reserved in the days of the silent pictures for that type of violinist who led the little movie-house orchestra. The perpetually used espressivo has become completely worn out. Even effective dramatic incidents are made trite by oversweet accompaniment or offensive over-exposition. A 'middle-ground,' objective musical type of interpretation that resorts to the espressivo only where it is really justified could by its economy greatly enhance the effectiveness of motion-picture music.

2
Function and Dramaturgy

The function of music in the cinema is one aspect – in an extreme version – of the general function of music under conditions of industrially controlled cultural consumption. Music is supposed to bring out the spontaneous, essentially human element in its listeners and in virtually all human relations. As the abstract art *par excellence,* and as the art farthest removed from the world of practical things, it is predestined to perform this function. The human ear has not adapted itself to the bourgeois rational and, ultimately, highly industrialized order as readily as the eye, which has become accustomed to conceiving reality as made up of separate things, commodities, objects that can be modified by practical activity. Ordinary listening, as compared to seeing, is 'archaic'; it has not kept pace with technological progress. One might say that to react with the ear, which is fundamentally a passive organ in contrast to the swift, actively selective eye, is in a sense not in keeping with the present advanced industrial age and its cultural anthropology.[1]

For this reason acoustical perception preserves comparably more traits of long bygone, pre-individualistic collectivities than optical perception. At least two of the most important elements of occidental music, the harmonic-contrapuntal one and that of its rhythmic articulation, point directly to a group modelled upon the ancient church community as its only possible inherent 'subject.' This direct relationship to a collectivity, intrinsic in the phenomenon itself, is probably connected with the sensations of spatial depth, inclusiveness, and absorption of individuality, which are common to all music.[2] But this very ingredient of collectivity, because of its essentially amorphous nature, leads itself to deliberate misuse for ideological purposes. Since music is antithetical to the definiteness of material things, it is also in opposition to the unambiguous distinctness of the concept. Thus it may easily serve as a means to create retrogression and confusion, all the more so because, despite its non-conceptual character, it is in other respects rationalized, extensively technified, and just as modern as it is archaic. This refers not only to the present methods of mechanical reproduction, but to the whole development of post-medieval music. Max Weber even terms the process of rationalization the historical principle according to which music developed. All middle-class music has an ambivalent character.[3] On the one hand, it is in a certain sense pre-capitalistic, 'direct,' a vague evocation of togetherness; on the other hand, because it has shared in the progress of civilization, it has become reified, indirect, and ultimately a 'means' among many others. This ambivalence determines its function under advanced capitalism. It is *par excellence* the medium in which irrationality can be practised rationally.

It has always been said that music releases or gratifies the emotions, but these emotions themselves have always been difficult to define. Their actual content seems to be only abstract opposition to prosaic existence. The greater the drabness of this existence, the sweeter the melody. The underlying need expressed by this inconsistency springs from the frustrations imposed on the masses of the people by social conditions. But this need itself is put into the service of commercialism. Because of its own rationality, so different from the way it is perceived, and its technical malleability, music can be made to serve regression 'psycho-technically' and in that role is more welcomed in proportion as it deceives its listeners in regard to the reality of everyday existence.

Such tendencies affect culture as a whole, but they manifest themselves with particular blatancy in music. The eye is always an organ of exertion, labour, and concentration; it grasps a definite object. The ear of the layman, on the other hand, as contrasted to that of the musical expert, is indefinite and passive. One does not have to open it, as one does the eye, compared to which it is indolent and dull. But this indolence is subject to the taboo that society imposes upon every form of laziness. Music as an art has always been an attempt to circumvent this taboo, to transform the indolence, dreaminess, and dullness of the ear into a matter of concentration, effort, and serious work. Today indolence is not so much overcome as it is managed and enhanced scientifically. Such a rationally planned irrationality is the very essence of the amusement industry in all its branches. Music perfectly fits the pattern.

The examples discussed below are opposed to this pattern. They are intended to show on what considerations any new attempts to solve the problems of musical dramaturgy, or the 'function' of music in motion pictures, are based. In order to emphasize the 'critical' ideas by means of which the existing stagnation can be overcome, drastic examples have been chosen, extreme instances that do not, however, preclude the possibility of a less pointed relationship between motion pictures and music. The musical solutions will be examined here solely from the point of view of dramaturgy, not that of purely musical structure and material. Each of these dramaturgic ideas permits of a variety of purely musical interpretations.

Sham Collectivity

A scene from *No Man's Land,* a pacifist picture by Victor Trivas, dating from 1930: A German carpenter receives the mobilization order of 1914. He locks his tool cupboard, takes down his knapsack, and, accompanied by his wife and children, crosses the street on the way to his barracks. A number of similar groups are shown. The atmosphere is melancholy, the pace is limp, unrhythmic. Music suggesting a military march is introduced quite softly. As it grows louder, the pace of the men becomes quicker, more rhythmic, more collectively unified. The women and children, too, assume a military bearing, and even the soldiers' mustaches begin to bristle. There follows a triumphant crescendo. Intoxicated by the music, the mobilized men, ready to kill and be killed, march into the barracks. Then, fade-out.

The dramaturgic clarification of this scene, the transformation of seemingly harmless individuals into a horde of barbarians, can be achieved only by resorting to music. Here music is not ornamental, but is essential to the meaning of the scene – and this is its dramaturgic justification. It does not merely produce an emotional atmosphere, for the accompanying picture makes this atmosphere fully apparent. The interpenetration of picture and music breaks through the conventional effect that usually connects both, because this very connection is explicitly represented, and then raised to critical awareness. Music is unveiled as the drug that it is in reality, and its intoxicating, harmfully irrational function becomes transparent. The composition and performance of the music combined with the picture must demonstrate to the public the destructive and barbarizing influence of such musical effects. The music must not be continually heroic, else the naive spectator would become intoxicated by it, like the men portrayed on the screen. Its heroism must appear as reflected, or to use Brecht's term, 'alienated.' In this case, the desired effect was achieved by overshrill instrumentation and harmonization with a tonality that constantly threatens to go wild.

Invisible Community

The closing scene of *Hangmen Also Die,* by Frltz Lang: Gestapo Chief Daluege is reading the official report on the shooting of the alleged assassin of Heydrich. According to this report, the Gestapo is well aware that the person in question is not the murderer, but a trusted Czech agent of the Gestapo, who has been 'framed' by the underground. Daluege signs the report after reading it carefully. The episode is quiet and matter-of-fact, but musically it is accompanied by a chorus and orchestra, which contrast sharply with the scene, performing a marching song in an animated tempo that increases dynamically from pianissimo to fortissimo. At the end, there is a *long shot* of the city of Prague, as though to show the real hero of the picture, the Czech people.

Here again the music acts as the representative of the collectivity: not the repressive collectivity drunk with its own power, but the oppressed invisible one, which does not figure in the scene. The music expresses this idea paradoxically by its dramatic distance from the scene. Its dramatic function here is the sensuous suggestion of something unsensuous: illegality.

Visible Solidarity

La Nouvelle Terre, 1933, a documentary film by Joris Ivens, showing the dredging of the Zuider Zee and its transformation into arable land: The picture includes a harvest scene in the fields newly conquered from the sea. But it does not end in triumph: the same people who have just harvested the grain are throwing it back into the sea. This incident took place during the economic depression of 1931, when foodstuffs were destroyed to prevent the collapse of the market. Only the end of the picture reveals the true meaning of its 'edifying' part. Those who drained the Zuider Zee are, viewed sociologically, identical with those who have to throw the food into the sea. Later the faces of the workers on the new land are seen in hunger demonstrations. The musical treatment of some episodes was designed to indicate this latent meaning of the whole picture, even during the dredging scenes. Twenty workmen are shown slowly transporting a huge steel conduit. They walk bent under their tremendous burden, their motions almost identical. The pressure and difficulty of their working conditions is transformed into solidarity by the music. To achieve this, the music could not confine itself to reproducing the 'mood' of the scene, a mood of gloom and great effort. This very mood had to be transcended. The score tried to make the incident meaningful by an austere and solemn theme. Although the rhythmical beat of the music synchronized with the work rhythm of the incident on the screen, the melody was rhythmically quite free and, strongly contrasting with the accompaniment, pointed beyond the constraint represented on the screen.

The following examples show how music, instead of limiting itself to conventional reinforcement of the action or mood, can throw its meaning into relief by setting itself in opposition to what is being shown on the screen.

Movement as a Contrast to Rest

Kuhle Wampe, by Brecht and Dudow, 1931: A slum district of drab, dilapidated suburban houses is shown in all its misery and filth. The atmosphere is passive, hopeless, depressing. The accompanying music is brisk, sharp, a polyphonic prelude of a marcato character, and its strict form 26 and stem tone, contrasted with the loose structure of the scenes, acts as a shock deliberately aimed at arousing resistance rather than sentimental sympathy.

Rest as a Contrast to Movement

In his *Outline for a New Musical Esthetics,* which contains many ideas for a new musical dramaturgy, Busoni cites the end of the second act of the *Tales of Hoffmann,* in the palace of the courtesan Giulietta, in which a bloody duel and the flight of the heroine with her hunchback lover are accompanied by the quiet tender rippling of the Barcarolle. By not participating in the action, the music expresses the cold indifference of the stars to human suffering, and is, as it were, congealed into a part of the scenery. Almost every motion picture affords an opportunity for such dramaturgic ideas.

Dans les Rues, 1933: The screen shows a bloody fight among young rowdies against the background of an early spring landscape. The music, in the form of variations, is tender, sad, rather remote; it expresses the contrast between the incident and the scene, without touching upon the action. Its lyrical character creates a distance from the savagery of the event: those who commit the brutalities are themselves victims.

Hangmen Also Die: A short scene shows Heydrich in a hospital bed, after the attempt on his life. He has a broken spine and is receiving a blood transfusion. There is a gloomy hospital atmosphere in the whole scene, which lasts only fourteen seconds. The attention of the spectator is centered on the dripping of the blood. The action is stalled, as it were, and for that reason the scene needs music. The most natural solution was to take the dripping of the blood as a point of departure. There could be no question of expressing the dying man's emotions or of duplicating the hospital atmosphere shown on the screen. Because Heydrich is a hangman, the musical formulation is a political issue; a German, fascist picture, by resorting to tragic and heroic music, could have transformed the criminal into a hero. The composer's task was to impart the true perspective of the scene to the spectator, and to bring out the significant point by brutal means. The dramatic solution was suggested associatively by the death of a rat. The music consists of brilliant, strident, almost elegant sequences, in a very high register, suggesting the German colloquial phrase *auf dem letzten Loch pfeifen* (literally, 'to blow through the last hole,' which corresponds to the English: 'to be on one's last legs'). The accompaniment figure is synchronized with the associative motive of the scene: the dripping of the blood is marked by a pizzicato in the strings and a piano figure in a high register.

The solution sought here is almost behavioristic. The music makes for adequate reactions on the part of the listeners and precludes the wrong associations.

Suspense and Interruption

Musical techniques for arousing suspense have been developed for the most part since the middle of the eighteenth century. The development of the orchestra crescendo by the Mannheim School paved the way and the Viennese Classicists and nineteenth-century Romanticists up to Strauss and Schonberg exploited these potentialities to the fullest. In this connection it is sufficient to mention the technique of dynamic pedal points – for instance, the transition from the third to the fourth movement of Beethoven's Fifth Symphony or the beginning of the Allegro of the *Leonore Overture* No. 3 – the false ending and extension of the 28 cadences. The possibility of resorting to such means of suspense in the cinema is only too obvious. Its music has stereotyped these means almost to the point of absurdity.

However, interruption, the complement and counterbalance of suspense, has been musically unexploited. In the drama, it plays a predominant role as episode or 'delaying action.' Interruptions are not extraneous to the drama; on the contrary, the antagonism between essence and appearance, of which the unfolding is the very core of drama, is deepened by the introduction of seemingly accidental elements that are not directly connected with the main action. One may think, say, of the monologue of the drunken watchman the morning after the murder of the king in *Macbeth.* Such interruptions could be particularly effective in motion-picture music.

For instance, in *Dans les Rues,* there is a scene showing a couple who have just declared their love for each other. The scene must be drawn out in order to show the genuineness of their emotion through little mannerisms of behavior, for the heroes are two young people who after their 'I love you' really have nothing to say; they are overwhelmed by the presence of love. In this case the crudest solution proved to be the most tender. The proprietress of the bistro sings a chanson. Its text has nothing whatever to do with the couple, but represents the love pangs of a servant girl who enumerates the different Paris subway stations at which she has waited in vain for her lover. This interruption gives the embarrassed young lovers an opportunity to smile.

In a conventional way, music is inserted episodically over and over again in all film revues and operettas. Their plots are repeatedly interrupted by songs and dances. In the present examples, however, the interruptions perform a dramatic function, by helping to master indirectly a situation that could not be directly unfolded as the main action.

A somewhat more general consideration of the form of the motion picture will cast light on such possibilities. The motion picture is a hybrid of the drama and the novel. Like the drama it presents persons and events directly, in the flesh, and the element of description does not intervene between the events and the spectator. Hence the requirement of 'intensity' in the motion picture, manifested as suspense, emotion, or conflict. On the other hand, an element of story-telling is inherent in the motion picture. Every feature film has to some extent the character of a pictorial reportage; it is articulated into chapters, rather than acts, and is built upon episodes. It is no accident that novels and stories can be more easily adapted to the screen than plays; aside from box-office considerations, this fact is directly related to the epic form of the motion picture. To be suitable for the screen, a play must be invested with novelistic features. But there is a disparity between the dramatic and the epic elements of the motion picture – its one-dimensional course and epic continuity detract from the intense concentration demanded by the dramatic quality of the events on the screen. This determines the objective task of music – it must at least replace, if not create, that intensity for the 'epic' parts. Music serves as the stop-gap for drama in the novel. Its illegitimate dramaturgic place is wherever intensity wanes and action assumes the form of exposition, which music alone can retranslate into direct presence.

Here is a simple illustration. The hero is walking home after a lovers' quarrel. Music is necessary to give intensity to this scene, which might otherwise fall flat. This function of music is clearest at points where the film jumps forward or backward in time, like a novel. When the passage of time must be expressed – and visually this is often done in a clumsy, mechanical fashion – music is needed to countaract the slackening of suspense. The story-telling element required to weld the plot and connect or separate the times and scenes of action, all that encumbering machinery of exposition and story-construction, are by music made more fluid and more intense and raised to the level of dramatic expression.

3
The New Musical Resources

As we pointed out earlier, there is a striking discrepancy between contemporary motion pictures and their musical accompaniment. Most often this accompaniment drifts across the screen like a haze, obscuring the visual sharpness of the picture and counteracting the realism for which in principle the film necessarily strives. It converts a kiss into a magazine cover, an outburst of unmitigated pain into a melodrama, a scene from nature into an oleograph. But all this could be dispensed with today because, in the course of the last few decades, autonomous music has developed new resources and techniques that really correspond to the technical requirements of the motion picture. Their use is urged not merely because they are 'timely'; it is not enough to demand only that the new motion-picture music should be new. The new musical resources should be used because objectively they are more appropriate than the haphazard musical padding with which motion pictures are satisfied today, and are superior to it.

We refer to the elements and techniques elaborated particularly in the works of Schönberg, Bartòk, and Stravinsky during the last thirty years. What is all-important in their music is not the increased number of dissonances, but the dissolution of the conventionalized musical idiom. In truly valid new music, everything is the direct result of the concrete requirement of structure, rather than of the tonal system or any ready-made pattern. A piece full of dissonances can be fundamentally conventional, while one based on comparatively simpler material can be absolutely novel if these resources are used according to the constructive requirements of the piece instead of the institutionalized flow of musical language. Even a sequence of triads can be unusual and striking when it does not follow the accustomed rot and is conceived only with regard to its specific meaning.

Music based on constructive principles, in which there is no room for clichés and embellishments, can be called 'objective' music, which is equivalent to the potentially objective music of the cinema.

The term 'objective' is susceptible to incorrect and narrow interpretation' such as, for instance, connecting it exclusively with musical neoclassicism, the 'functional' stylistic ideal as developed by Stravinsky and his followers. But advanced motion-picture music need not necessarily be cold. Under certain circumstances, the dramaturgic function of the accompanying music can consist precisely in breaking through the soberly objective surface of the picture and releasing latent suspense. We do not mean that the musician, in composing objective motion-picture music, must assume a detached attitude, but that he must deliberately choose the musical elements required by the context instead of succumbing to musical clichés and prefabricated emotionalism. The musical material must be perfectly subordinated to the given dramatic task. The development of modern music tends in the same direction.[1] As intimated above, it can be regarded as a process of rationalization in so far as every single musical element is at each moment derived from the structure of the whole. But as music becomes more pliable through its own structural principles, it also becomes more pliable for purposes of application to other media. The release of new types of resources, which was denounced as anarchistic and chaotic, actually led to the establishment of principles of construction far more strict and comprehensive than those known to traditional music. These principles make it possible always to choose the exact means required by a particular subject at a particular moment, and there is therefore no need to use formal means unsuitable for a specific purpose. Thus it has become possible to do full justice to the ever-changing problems and situations of the motion picture.

It is easy to see that the traditional resources long since frozen into automatic associations cannot achieve this, although even they can be used meaningfully again if they are clarified and 'alienated' in the light of advanced practice. Here are a few instances of these petrified associations: A 4/4 bar with regular accents on the strong beats always has a military or triumphal character; the succession of the first and third steps of the scale, played piano, in a quiet tempo, because of its modal character suggests something religious; an accented 3/4 bar suggests the waltz and gratuitous *joie de vivre*. Such associations often place the events of the film in a false perspective. The new musical resources prevent this. The listener is stimulated to grasp the scene in itself; he not only hears the music, but also sees the picture from a fresh point of view. True, the new music does not represent conceptually mediated ideas, as is the case with programmatic music, in which waterfalls rustle and sheep bleat. But it can exactly reflect the tone of a scene, the specific emotional situation, the degree of seriousness or casualness, significance or inconsequence, sincerity or falseness – differences not within the possibilities of the conventional Romantic techniques.

In a French puppet film of 1933 there was an ensemble scene – a board meeting of industrial magnates – which required a benevolently satirical accompaniment. The score that was submitted, despite its puppet-like thinness, appeared to be so aggressive and 'critical' in its use of advanced musical resources that the industrialists who had commissioned the picture rejected it and ordered another.

The 'non-objectivity' of epigonous music is inseparable from its seeming antithesis, its cliché character. Only because definite musical configurations become patterns that are resorted to over and over again can these configurations be automatically associated with certain expressive values and in the end seem to be 'expressive' in themselves. The new music avoids such patterns, meeting specific requirements with ever-new configurations, and as a result expression can no longer be hypostatized and made independent of the purely musical content.

The suitability of modern, unfamiliar resources should be recognized from the standpoint of the motion picture itself. The fact is that this form of drama originated in the county fair and the cheap melodrama has left traces that are still apparent; sensation is its very life element. This is not to be understood solely in a negative sense, as lack of taste and aesthetic discrimination; only by using the element of surprise can the motion picture give everyday life, which it claims to reproduce by virtue of its technique, an appearance of strangeness, and disclose the essential meaning beneath its realistic surface. More generally, the drudgery of life as depicted in a reportage can become dramatic only through sensational presentation, which to a certain extent negates everyday life through exaggeration, and, when artistically true, reveals tensions that are 'blacked out' in the conventional concept of 'normal' average existence. The horrors of sensational literary and cinematic trash lay bare part of the barbaric foundation of civilization. To the extent that the motion picture in its sensationalism is the heir of the popular horror story and dime novel and remains below the established standards of middle-class art, it is in a position to shatter those standards, precisely through the use of sensation, and to gain access to collective energies that are inaccessible to sophisticated literature and painting. It is this very perspective that cannot be reached with the means of traditional music. But modern music is suitable to it. The fear expressed in the dissonances of Schönberg's most radical period far surpasses the measure of fear conceivable to the average middle-class individual; it is a historical fear, a sense of impending doom.

Something of this fear is alive in the great sensational films, for instance in the scene of the collapsing roof in the night club (*San Francisco*), or in *King Kong* when the giant gorilla hurls a New York elevated train down into the street. The traditional music written for such scenes has never been remotely adequate to them, whereas the shocks of modern music, by no means an accidental consequence of its technological rationalization – still unassimilated after thirty years – could meet their requirements. Schönberg's music for an imaginary film, *Begleitmusik zu einer Lichtspielszene,* op. 34, full of a sense of fear, of looming danger and catastrophe, is a landmark pointing the way for the full and accurate use of the new musical resources. Naturally the extension of their expressive potentialities is applicable not only to the realm of fear and horror; in the opposite direction, too, that of extreme tenderness, ironic detachment, empty waiting, and unfettered power, the new musical resources can explore fields inaccessible to traditional resources because these latter present themselves as something that has always been known, and therefore are deprived in advance of the power to express the unfamiliar and unexplored.

For example, *Hangmen Also Die,* after the preliminary music, begins by showing a large portrait of Hitler in a banquet hall of the Hradshin Castle. As the portrait appears, the music stops on a penetrating widespread chord containing ten different tones. Hardly any traditional chord has the expressive power of this extremely advanced sonority. The twelve-tone chord at the moment of Lulu's death in Berg's opera produces an effect very much like that of a motion picture. While the cinema technique aims essentially at creating extreme tension, traditional music, with the slight dissonances it allows, knows of no equivalent material. But suspense is the essence of modern harmony, which knows no chord without an inherent 'tendency' toward further action, while most of the traditional chords are self-sufficient. Moreover, even those traditional harmonies that are charged with specific dramatic associations have long since become so tame that they are no more capable of giving an idea of the chaotic and fearful present-day reality than nineteenth-century verse forms are capable of giving an idea of fascism. To make this clear it is enough to imagine an extreme case, such as the picture of the explosion of a block buster, accompanied by conventional martial music in the style of Meyerbeer or Verdi. The modern motion picture, in its most consistent productions, aims at unmetaphorical contents that are beyond the range of stylization. This requires musical means that do not represent a stylized picture of pain, but rather its tonal record. This particular dimension of the new musical resources was made apparent by Stravinsky in his *Sacre du Printemps*.

Here are, briefly stated, some of the specifically musical elements suitable to the motion-picture:

Musical Form

Most motion pictures use short musical forms. The length of a musical form is determined by its relation to the musical material. Tonal music of the last two and a half centuries favored relatively long, developed forms. Consciousness of a tonal centre can be achieved only by parallel episodes, developments, and repetitions that require a certain amount of time. No tonal incident in the sense of major/minor tonality is intelligible as such; it becomes 'tonal' only by means of relationships revealed in the course of a more or less extensive whole. This tendency increases with the specific weight of the modulations, and the further the music moves away from the original tonality, the more time it needs to re-establish its tonal center of gravity. Thus all tonal music necessarily contains an element of the 'superfluous,' because each theme, in order to fulfil its function in the system of reference, must be expressed more often than would be required according to its own meaning. The short romantic forms (Chopin and Schumann) contradict this only in appearance. The expressive power of certain aphoristic instrumental compositions of these masters is based on their fragmentary, unfinished, suggestive character, and they never claim to be complete or 'closed.'

The brevity of the new music is fundamentally different. In it, the individual musical episodes and the patterns of the themes are conceived without regard to a pre-arranged system of reference. They are not intended to be 'repeatable' and require no repetition, but stand by themselves. If they are expanded, it is not by means of symmetrical devices, such as sequences or resumptions of the first part of a song form, but rather by means of a developing variation of the given original materials, and it is not necessary that these should be easily recognizable. All this results in a condensation of the musical form that goes far beyond the romantic fragments. Instances of this are Schönberg's piano pieces op. 11 and 19, and his monodrama *Erwartung;* Stravinsky's pieces for string quartet and his Japanese songs; and the works of Anton Webern. It is obvious that modern music is especially qualified to construct consistent precise short forms, which contain nothing superfluous, which come to the point at once, and which need no expansion for architectonic reasons.

Musical Profiles

The emancipation of each motive or theme from symmetry and the necessity of repetition makes it possible to formulate specific musical ideas in a far more drastic and penetrating fashion, and to free the individual musical events from all unessential gewgaws. In the new music there is no room for padding.

It is because of this capacity for unfettered characterization that the new music is in keeping with the prose character of the motion picture. At the same time this sharpening of musical characterization permits a sharpness of expression, which the 'stylization' of the elements of the traditional music made impossible. While traditional music always preserves a certain restraint in the expression of sorrow, grief, and fear, the new style tends to be unrestrained. Sorrow can turn into appalling despair, repose into glassy rigidity, fear into panic. But the new music is also capable of expressing absence of expression, quietude, indifference, and apathy with an intensity beyond the power of traditional music. Impassiveness has been known in music only since Eric Satie, Stravinsky, and Hindemith.

The range of expression has been widened not only with regard to the different types of musical profiles but above all to their alternation. Traditional music, with the exception of the technique of surprise used, for instance, by Berlioz and Richard Strauss, usually requires a certain amount of time for the alternation of themes, and the necessity of achieving an adjusted balance between the tonalities and the symmetrical parts prevents the immediate juxtaposition of themes according to their own meaning. As a rule, the new music no longer recognizes such considerations, and can fashion its forms by means of the sharpest contrasts. The new musical language can satisfy the technical principle of abrupt change elaborated by the motion picture because of its inherent flexibility.

Dissonance and Polyphony

For the layman, the most striking feature of the new musical language is its wealth of discords, namely the simultaneous employment of intervals such as the minor second and the major seventh and the formation of chords of six or more different notes. Although the wealth of dissonances in modern music is a superficial characteristic, far less significant than the structural changes of the musical language) it involves an element of especial importance for the motion picture. Sound is robbed of its static quality and made dynamic by the ever-present factor of the 'unresolved.' The new language is dramatic even prior to the 'conflict,' the thematic development with its explicit antagonisms. A similar feature is inherent in the motion picture. The principle of tension is latently so active even in the weakest productions that incidents which of themselves are credited with no importance whatsoever appear like scattered fragments of a meaning that the whole is intended to clarify and that transcend themselves. The new musical language is particularly well-suited to do justice to this element of the motion picture.[2]

The emancipation of harmony also supplies the corrective for the requirement discussed in the chapter on prejudices: melody at any price. In traditional music, this requirement is not altogether meaningless, because the independence of its other elements, particularly harmony, is so restricted that the center of gravity inevitably lies in the melody, which is itself guided by harmony. But for that very reason the melodic element has become conventionalized and outworn, while the emancipated harmony of today unburdens the overworked melodic element, and paves the way for ideas and characteristic turns in the vertical, non-melodic dimension.' It also helps to combat melodizing in another way. The conventional notion of melody means melody in the highest voice, which, borrowed from the *Lied* style, is supposed to occupy the foreground of the listener's attention. Melody of this type is a figure, not a background. But in the motion picture the foreground is the scene projected on the screen, and permanent accompaniment of this scene with a melody in the highest voice must of necessity lead to obscurity, blurring, and confusion. The liberation of harmony and the conquest of a genuine polyphonic freedom, which is not reduced to academic conventional techniques of imitation, permits the music to function as a background in another sense than that of a mere backdrop of noise, and to add to the true melody of the picture, namely the action portrayed, meaningful illustrations and genuine contrasts. These decisive potentialities of motion-picture music can be realized only by the use of the new musical resources, and so far have not even been seriously considered.

Dangers of the New Style

The elimination of the familiar frame of reference of traditional music results in a number of dangers. First of all, there is the irresponsible use of the new resources in a hit-or-miss style, modernism in the bad sense of the word, that is to say, the use of advanced media for their own sake, not because the subject calls for them. A poor piece composed in the traditional musical language can easily be recognized as such by any more or less trained musician or layman. The unconventional character of the new musical language and its remoteness from what is taught in the conservatories make the recognition of stupidity and pretentious bungling in modern music more difficult for the average listener, although objectively such bungling can as well be spotted as it could before. For instance, certain novices might be ready to exhaust the listener with completely absurd twelve-tone compositions which seem advanced, whereas their sham radicalism would only weaken the effect of the motion picture. It is true that this danger is today far more acute in autonomous music than in motion-picture music, but the demand for new composers might lead to a situation in which the cause of new music will be so badly represented that the trash of the old guard will triumph.

The methods of new music imply new dangers that even experienced composers must take into consideration: excessive complexity of detail; the mania for making every moment of the accompanying music arresting; pedantry; formalistic trifling. Especially dangerous is the hasty adoption of the twelve-tone technique, which can degenerate into a mechanical task and in which the arithmetical consistency of the sequence is supposed to replace the genuine consistency of the musical whole – resulting in no consistency at all.

While it is unlikely that the motion-picture industry, organized as it is today, will permit wild experiments on the expensive medium of motion pictures, another danger is much more imminent. The defects of conventional motion-picture music are generally realized, more or less consciously, yet radical innovations are largely excluded for commercial reasons. As a result, a certain tendency to follow a middle course is beginning to make itself felt; the ominous demand: modern, but not too much so, is heard in several quarters. Certain modern techniques, like the ostinato of the Stravinsky school, have begun to sneak in, and the abandonment of the routine threatens to give rise to a new pseudo-modern routine. The industry encourages this tendency within certain limits, while at the same time composers who have adopted the modern idiom, but who do not want or cannot afford to spoil their chances on the market, tend to work for the industry. The hope that an advanced and original musical language can impose itself by the detour of false moderate imitations is illusory; such compromises destroy the meaning of the new language, rather than propagate it.

4
Sociological Aspects

In his painstaking and informative study, *Film Music*,[1] Kurt London has collected the data of the history of motion-picture music. It would be superfluous to repeat the facts here; however, it is pertinent to inquire whether the historical approach is applicable to motion-picture music; and to analyze the significance of the developmental phases outlined by London. One can hardly speak of a genuine history of motion-picture music, even in the dubious sense in which this term is generally used: that is, to imply that any form of art has an autonomous history. Up until now motion-picture music has not developed according to its own laws and has hardly taken cognizance of problems and solutions posed by the nature of its own material. The changes it has undergone relate to some extent to methods of mechanical reproduction and to some extent represent ill-considered, clumsy, and backward attempts to pander to the imagined or actual taste of the public. While it is reasonable to speak of a qualitatively progressive development, for instance, from Edison's apparatus to the modern sound picture, it would be naive to speak of a roughly corresponding artistic development from the *Kinothek* to the musical scores of modern sound tracks.

The haphazard development of cinema music is comparable to that of the radio or of the motion picture itself. It is first of all a question of personnel. In the early days of the amusement industry, owners and directors were the same persons. Experts were used far less than in the older industries, either in the administration as a whole or in the individual production groups, and as a result a pioneer spirit of incompetence prevailed. What is true of motion pictures and the radio also holds true for motion-picture music: the artistic level of these media was determined by those who first entered the field, attracted by the commercial prospects of the new ventures. Motion-picture music, however, suffers from a particular handicap: from the very beginning it has been regarded as an auxiliary art not of first-rank importance. In the early days it was entrusted to anyone who happened to be around and willing – often enough to musicians whose qualifications were not such as to permit them to compete in fields where solid musical standards still obtained. This created an affinity between inferior 'hack' musicians, busybodies, and motion-picture music.

In order to understand the personnel problem of cinema music, some more general reflections on the sociology of the musician may be appropriate. The whole realm of musical performance has always had the social stigma of a service for those who can pay. The practice of music is historically linked with the idea of selling one's talent, and even one's self, directly, without intermediaries, rather than selling one's labor in its congealed form, as a commodity; and through the ages the musician, like the actor, has been regarded as closely akin to the lackey, the jester, or the prostitute. Although musical performance presupposes the most exacting labor, the fact that the artist appears in person, and the coincidence between his existence and his achievement, together create the illusion that he does it for fun, that he earns his living without honest labor, and this very illusion is readily exploited.

Before the jazz age, most people used to look with contempt at a musician who led a dance orchestra. This deprecating glance is the rudiment of an attitude that has to some extent shaped the social character of musicians. In the early bourgeois era musicians were called in from the servants' quarters where even Haydn had to take his meals, and were subject to the laws of competition. But the taint of social outcasts still clings to them. Even the austere chamber-music player sometimes assumes the posture of an obsequious and resentful head-waiter who hopes for a tip. Even he still takes note of the ladies and gentlemen of the audience, and ingratiates himself by the sweetness of his playing and the smoothness of his manners. His turned-up coat collar, the violin under his arm and the studied carelessness of his appearance remind his audience of his colleagues of the cafe, from whose ranks he has often come.[2]

Some of the best qualities of musical reproduction, its spontaneity, its sensuousness, its aspect of vagrancy opposed to settled orderliness – in short, everything that is good in the much-abused notion of the itinerant musician – is reflected in the popular picture of the gypsy. If this picture were eradicated, musical performance, too, would probably come to an end, just as, if complete technical rationalization were achieved and if music could really be 'drawn' rather than written down in symbols, the function of the interpreter, the intermediary, would merge with that of the composer who 'produces' music.

At the same time, the habit of rendering 'service' – in Germany, orchestra players speak of *Abenddienst*, evening service – has left ominous marks on musicians. Among these is the mania to please, even at the price of self-humiliation, manifested in a thousand ways that range from over-elegant dress to zealous pandering to what the audience wants. This conformism of professional musicians shackles modern composition even more than the passivity of the concert-goers. There remains also a very special and anachronistic kind of envy and malice, and a fondness for intrigue, the disreputable heritage of a profession only superficially adjusted to competitive conditions. It is such archaic features that fit paradoxically into the trend of musical mass culture, which does away with competition, while still needing the old-fashioned gypsy-like traits as an added attraction. A servility both coquettish and impudent is useful for ensnaring the customer; intrigue and the irresistible urge to deceive one's colleagues, often combined with insincere 'comradeship,' harmonize with the more pragmatic role of business. The musicians in control have a spontaneous understanding of the aims and practices of the amusement industry. In fact, the late-comer industry of motion pictures has not rid itself of the pre-capitalist elements of musicianship, the social type of the *Stehgeiger*,[3] despite its apparent contradiction to industrial production and the artistic incompetence of its outspoken representatives. On the contrary, this 'irrational' type itself has been given a monopolistic position in the streamlined set-up. The industry, out of deepest kinship, has attracted him, preferred him to all musicians with objective tendencies, and made him a permanent institution. He has been regimented like other sham elements of a former spontaneity. The cinema exploits the barber aspect of his personality as a Don Juan, and his head-waiter functions as a troubadour deluxe, and occasionally even gives him the role of a bouncer to keep undesirable elements out. Its musical ideal is *schmaltz* in a chrome metal pot. But since the regimentation of the gypsy musician deprives him of the last vestiges of spontaneity which the inexorable technical and organizational machinery has already undermined, objectively nothing is left of the itinerant musician except a few bad mannerisms of performance.

Under these circumstances, it is preposterous to use words such as 'history' with reference to an apocryphal branch of art like motion-picture music. The person who around 1910 first conceived the repulsive idea of using the Bridal March from *Lohengrin* as an accompaniment is no more of a historical figure than any other second-hand dealer. Similarly, the prominent composer of today who, under the pretext of motion-picture requirements, willingly or unwillingly debases his music earns money, but not a place in history. The historical processes that can be perceived in cinema music are only reflections of the decay of middle-class cultural goods into commodities for the amusement market. At most, one can say that music has parasitically shared in the progress of the technical resources and the growing wealth of the motion-picture industry. It would be ludicrous to claim that motion-picture music has really evolved, either in itself or in its relation to other motion-picture media.

Musical Administration

This does not mean that motion-picture music has stood still. On the contrary, the economic might of the industry has set a tremendously dynamic machinery in motion. There is a constant stream of improvements of all kinds: new composers, new ideas in the sense of gadgets, marketable tricks that are sufficiently different from earlier ones to be conspicuous, yet not different enough to offend established habits. But what is true of all mass cultural advances under the prevailing system is true in this instance, too: ostentatious spending has increased, and the mode of presentation, the technique of transmission in the broadest sense, from acoustical accuracy to the psycho-technical treatment of the audience, has been improved in direct proportion to the capital invested, but nothing essential has changed in the music itself, its substance, its material, its function as a whole, or in the quality of the compositions. There has only been a streamlining of the facade. The progress is one of means, not of ends.

There is a striking disproportion between the tremendous improvement in the technique of recording, on which all the miracles of this technique are spent, and the music itself, either indifferent or borrowed without taste or logic from the stock of clichés. Formerly the movie theatre pianist thumped out the *Lohengrin* Bridal Chorus in the semi-darkness; today, after the extermination of the pianist, the Bridal Chorus, or its made-to-order equivalent, is projected in neon lights of a hundred different colours, but it is still the old Bridal Chorus, and the moment it resounds everyone knows that lawful wedded bliss is being glorified. The triumphant procession from the *Kinothek* to the movie palace has really been marking time.

If there is such a thing as a historical phase of motion-picture music, it is marked by the transition of the industry from more or less important private capitalistic enterprises to highly concentrated and rationalized companies, which divide the market among themselves and control it, although they fondly imagine that they are obeying its laws. This transition was accomplished before the development of pictures with sound, according to Kurt London, between 1913 and 1928. It might be placed in the early 'twenties, when the first big movie palaces were built, when the custom of the 'opening night' was deliberately grafted on the cinema in a strenuous effort to make it a social event, and when deluxe 'super-productions' were first promoted with the aid of extensive national and international advertising. The musical equivalent of these innovations was the replacement of the inconspicuous little group of musicians, such as is used in cafes, by the symphony orchestras of the great moving-picture theatres.

The full-fledged and quantitatively pretentious scores composed for the last silent pictures were essentially the same as those composed later for sound pictures. They merely had to be recorded, as it were, and synchronized with the speaking parts. Kurt London comments on this stage:

> Finally, in the last few years of the silent film period, the big cinema palaces were served by orchestras which, composed, as they were, of 50–100 musicians, put to shame many a medium sized city orchestra. Parallel with this development, a new career for conductors offered itself: they had to lead the cinema orchestra and select the illustrative music. Prominent men often filled these posts with salaries which more often than not exceeded those of an opera conductor.[4]

The term 'prominent' as used here does not express real artistic accomplishments, but is part of the grandiloquent phraseology affected by all advertising in the entertainment industry, with its insincere slogan that nothing is too good for the public. This kind of prominence is determined by the fabulous salaries paid to those whom the publicity agencies elect to build up – the prominence of Radio City, the Pathé Theatre in Paris, or the Ufapalast am Zoo in Berlin. It belongs to the realm that Siegfried Kracauer called *Angestelltenkultur*, culture[5] of the white-collar workers, of supposedly high-class entertainment, accessible to recipients of small pay checks, yet presented in such a way that nothing seems too good or too expensive for them. It is a pseudo-democratic luxury, which is neither luxurious nor democratic, for the people who walk on heavily carpeted stairways into the marble palaces and glamorous castles of moviedom are incessantly frustrated without being aware of it. This kind of opulence, manifested, for instance, in submersible and floodlighted monster orchestras, marks the beginning of a development that has left behind it all the obvious naïveté of the old amusement park, but raised the technique of the barker to the point of anonymous yet all-embracing practice.

This development, however, is not merely a quantitative one. The careful planning and sumptuous presentation of motion-picture music has changed its social purpose. Its inflated power and dimensions ostentatiously and directly demonstrate the economic power behind it. Its rich display of colours masks the monotony of serial productions. Its excessive ebullience and optimism enhance its universal advertising appeal. Music thus becomes one of the departments of cultural industry.

The administrative element was inherent in cinema music from the very beginning. The time beater who selected the pieces, the editor of the *Kinothek* and the arranger have always thumbed through the treasury of traditional music as through a stock of standard goods, and chosen what best suited their purpose. The summary way in which they handled the cultural riches at their disposal, utilizing 'Asleep in the Deep' or the fate theme of *Carmen* according to the circumstances, was always that of the bureaucrat who finally divests works of art of all their meaning and brings them down to the status of auxiliary means designed to produce a predetermined effect. Today this attitude has become all-pervasive. It is as though the process of rationalization of art and the conscious command of its resources were diverted by social forces from the real purpose of art, and directed merely toward 'making friends and influencing people.' Progress has become perverted into calculating the audience's reactions, and the result is a combination of third-rate entertainment, maudlin sentimentality, and boastful advertisements of what is going to be shown.

In earlier motion-picture music, bureaucratic manipulation was mitigated by overt barbarism – then no fiction of taste invested the mutilated melodies with the glamour of intellectual achievement, and no highly complicated machine put itself between the music and its effect on the public. The pianist who played 'Asleep in the Deep' when the ship went down on the silent screen, coloured in brown or green for the occasion, and even the small orchestra that pandered to the maharajah's favorite wife by playing an exotic medley when she walked down the stairs were doubtless also employees free from any artistic scruples; but they understood their audiences and were not too different from them; they were not completely subjected to their superiors, and still had in them something of the ribaldry and lust for adventure that characterized the county fairs in which the moving-picture theatres originated. It is this 'illegitimate,' still impromptu and anarchistic element that motion pictures as big business drove out of their music. And it is this 'purge' that is called progress, and doubtless *is* progress as far as wealth of resources and planning of their distribution is concerned. But such progress is of dubious value. Since its streamlining, cinema music has become a helpless victim of culture without becoming one whit more cultured than it was before it attained respectability. Its progress consists only in the fact that trash was taken out of its humble hiding place and set up as an official institution.

Stagnation

Subjection to administrative control is responsible for the stagnation of motion-picture music. The catalogue and pigeon-hole treatment of musical material automatically results in the tendency to confine it to the existing supply, and, whenever anything new emerges, in the attempt to mould it to fit administrative classifications. No more than any other department of bureaucratized culture does music leave any room for the freedom or fantasy of the artist, and even when, more or less for considerations of prestige, so-called creative minds are called in, they are engaged on such terms that they either comply at once with prevailing standards or are taught by the businessmen and their representatives in the industry to produce, with more or less resistance, what everybody else produces. To be sure, the difference between the trained musical expert and the amateurish old-timer can still be felt, but it tends to disappear – the old-timers will eventually die off, and the experts will behave like the old-timers. Up to now attempts to induce the most important European composers, Schönberg and Stravinsky, to write for motion pictures have failed. Any other eminent musician who wants to crash the gates of the studios in order to make a living is forced to make concessions that are not justified by the objective requirements of the industry, although these requirements are invoked as an excuse.

Everyone is subject to the same pressure, which produces the harmony between the system and its executive organs. The statement frequently made that *avant-garde* composers have a deep interest in moving pictures and are attracted by the technical novelty of the medium is false. The Baden-Baden Music Festival, where experiments in cinema music were first undertaken, tried in a pretentious fashion to glorify the dubious concept of *Gebrauchskunst*, or commercial art, but Baden-Baden is not Hollywood, which decided these matters long ago with unself-conscious candor. The only result of the experiments with 'mechanical music' was that a few composers were encouraged to enter the new market and rationalized their adjustment to it as an advanced achievement of the technocratic spirit. The truth is that no serious composer writes for the motion pictures for any other than money reasons; and in the studios he does not feel that he is a beneficiary of utopian technical potentialities, but a regimented employee who can be discharged on any pretext.[6]

Since independent composers have lost their old economic base and are now forced to give up even their last footholds, it would be both sentimental and heartless to blame anyone for making a living by writing commercial music. However, no one should invoke the alleged spirit of the times to foster ideologies designed to comfort himself and his employers. The composer working under duress should rather try to impose as much novel music as possible, contrary to the prevailing practice, in the hope, however feeble, that he will thus help to improve the standards of the whole industry.

It would be superficial, however, to explain the stagnation of motion-picture music on the basis of personnel. The present distribution of positions of musical importance is only a tangible symptom of the social laws to which the whole system is subject. The rationalization of the motion picture is identical with its complete subordination to the producers' idea of the effect it will make on the public, and it is this fact which cuts off any possibility of a real development of cinema music. Only music rated as 'sure-fire box office' is accepted, and is refers not only to effectiveness in general, but to highly specific and thousandfold tested effects in specific situations. Because, for real or pretended reasons of economy, no risks are permitted, the industry accepts only material similar to that which has already proved its market value. The art directors in the service of the mammoth concerns conform to the aesthetic verdict pronounced during the final phases of free competition.

This explains the present situation. For at the time when motion-picture music was in its rudimentary stage, the breach between middle-class audiences and the really serious music which expressed the situation of the middle classes had become unbridgeable. This breach can be traced back as far as *Tristan,* a work that has probably never been understood and liked as much as *Aïda, Carmen,* or even the *Meistersinger.* The operatic theatre became finally estranged from its audience between 1900 and 1910, with the production of *Salome* and *Electra,* the two advanced operas of Richard Strauss. The fact that after 1910, with the *Rosenkavalier* – it is no accident that this opera has been made into a moving picture – he turned to a retrospective stylized way of writing reflects his awareness of that breach. Strauss was one of the first to attempt to bridge the gap between culture and the audience, by selling out culture.

Since Strauss, all really modern music has been driven into the esoteric. Throughout the world, the taste of the public, particularly the operatic audiences, has become static and no longer tolerates anything new. This stagnation is perhaps more pronounced in America than elsewhere, for reasons such as the special position of the Metropolitan Opera, indicative of the absence of a musical tradition with an old audience and the innumerable channels of musical erudition that existed in Europe; insufficient familiarity with the old works acts as an obstacle to the acceptance of the new.

The practitioners of commercial music must reckon with this state of affairs. They have had to deal with an illiterate, intolerant, and uncritical public taste, and they have had to bow to it if they wanted to remain true to their dubious maxim: give the public nothing but what the public wants. The contradiction between the middle-class public and its music was resolved in antipathy against anything experimental, anything that is even remotely suspected of being intellectual, and even anything that is just different. The overlords of the motion pictures have made the public judgment their own, and even outdo it by the provocative display of their authority. Motion-picture music has no history, because even before the rise of the motion picture, opera and concert audiences resented their artistic development whenever it touched sensitive spots, or whenever it contradicted the ideal of relaxation and amusement in a thoroughly 'rationalized' society. Motion-picture music only denies to the listener what he refuses to listen to in any case.

The motion pictures are made to measure for their customers, planned according to their real or supposed needs, and reproduce these needs. But at the same time the products that are most widespread, and therefore closest to the public, are objectively most remote from the public, as regards the methods by which they are produced and the interests they represent. Motion-picture production is entirely divorced from that living contact with the audience, which is still operative in every stage performance; the alleged will of the public is manifested only indirectly, through the box-office receipts, that is to say, in a completely reified form.

The contradiction between universal directness and unbridgeable remoteness marks the weak link in the planning of the effect, to which everything is subordinated. To conceal this weakness is one of the main purposes of manipulation, and indeed one of the most important elements of the effect itself. Hence, along with exaggerated advertising, the importance of the movie magazines, the movie columns in the newspapers, and the syndicated gossip that transforms even the intimacy of private life into an appendage of the movie machinery.

It is to this sphere that motion-picture music belongs socially. It is not only an element of the manufactured general irrationality, the so-called relaxation that is intended to mask the heartlessness of late industrial society by late industrial techniques; it also, more specifically, brings the picture close to the public, just as the picture brings itself close to it by means of the close-up. It attempts to interpose a human coating between the reeled-off pictures and the spectators. Its social function is that of a cement, which holds together elements that otherwise would oppose each other unrelated – the mechanical product and the spectators, and also the spectators themselves. The old stage theatre, too, was confronted with a similar need, as soon as the curtain went down. Music between the acts met that need. Cinema music is universalized between-the-acts music, but used also and precisely when there is something to be seen. It is the systematic fabrication of the atmosphere for the events of which it is itself part and parcel. It seeks to breathe into the pictures some of the life that photography has taken away from them.[7] Not for nothing did music migrate from the orchestra pit to the screen, of which it has become an integral part. It works on the spectator together with the picture strips. Manipulated comfort has been transformed into human interest, and in the end it is nothing but another ingredient of that universal advertising into which the pictures themselves tend to develop.

Today, the roar of MGM's lion reveals the secret of all motion-picture music: a feeling of triumph that the motion picture and motion-picture music have become a reality. The music sets the tone of the enthusiasm the picture is supposed to whip up in the audience. Its basic form is the fanfare, and the ritual of musical 'titles' shows this unmistakably. Its action is advertising, and nothing else. It points with unswerving agreement to everything that happens on the screen, and creates the illusion that the effect that is to be achieved by the whole picture has already been achieved. Occasionally, by the use of standardized configurations, it interprets the meaning of the action for the less intelligent members of the audience, somewhat in the way patent medicines are promoted by means of pseudo-scientific explanations. The whole form language of current cinema music derives from advertising. The motif is the slogan; the instrumentation, the standardized picturesque; the accompaniments to animated cartoons are advertising jokes; and sometimes it is as though the music replaced the names of the commercial articles that the motion pictures do not yet dare mention directly.

It is impossible to predict where all this will lead. Thus, it would be a real Hollywood idea that could be expressed in dollars and cents to give each actor his personal advertising leitmotif, to be heard every time he makes an appearance. The basic structure of all advertising: the division into conspicuous pictures or words and the inarticulate background also characterizes motion-picture music. It is either a hit or an amorphous sound, made up of senseless sequences of triplets which are contemptuously called 'noodles' in the jargon of the studios. There is nothing in it other than tunes that can at once be picked up and remembered by the audience, and a vague droning of imperceptible harmonies.

The collective function of music has become transformed into the function of ensnaring the customer. But ultimately, the subordination of everything to the advertising effect may well defeat its own purpose. The hits have become so trite in order to be easily remembered that they can no longer be remembered at all. The omnipresent advertising and the sugar-coated crooning grow tiresome, and the effect they arouse is indifference, if not open resistance. Thus, in the musical field, too, industrial rationalization ultimately proves to be what it has long since become in the economic field: its own enemy. Even according to the standards of the industry, motion-picture music should be fundamentally changed. But the same industrial standards make such a change impossible.

5
Elements of Aesthetics

To establish aesthetic principles of cinema music is as dubious an enterprise as to write its history. Up until now all attempts at an aesthetic analysis of motion pictures and radio, the two most important media of the cultural industry, have been more or less formalistic. The rule of big business has fettered the freedom of artistic creation, which is the prerequisite for a fruitful interaction between form and content; and a concrete aesthetics must necessarily refer to such an interaction. Because of the vulgar materialism of the content of motion pictures entirely alien to art, aesthetic considerations about them so far had to dodge the whole issue of content. That is why they have only been abstract. They have dealt predominantly with technicalities such as the laws of movement or colour, the sequence, the cutting, or with vague categories such as 'the inner rhythm.' Although the criteria derived from such analyses can to some extent circumscribe the framework of *métier* within a given production, they are completely insufficient to determine whether the product is good or bad. It is possible to imagine a motion picture – and this applies to its music as well – which conforms to all these criteria, upon which an enormous amount of conscientious labor and expert knowledge has been spent, and which is nevertheless utterly devoid of any real value, because the falseness and emptiness of the underlying conception have degraded the formal achievements into merely technical ingredients.

Quite apart from the detrimental influence of commercialism, aesthetic analyses of the motion picture easily become inadequate because it is rooted less in artistic wants than in the fact that in the twentieth century optical and acoustic technique reached a definite stage, which is essentially unrelated, or related only very indirectly, to any possible aesthetic idea. An attempt to formulate the aesthetic laws of the Greek tragedy, for instance, might be based on concrete social and historical factors, such as the symbolic rites of the Greek religion, the sacrifice, the trial, the primitive family conflicts, and the dawning critical attitude toward mythology. To attempt anything of this kind with regard to the motion picture would be puerile. Its connection with the developmental tendencies of dramatic or novelistic art is defined only by the fact that it takes for granted and assimilates these traditional forms, that is to say, reproduces them with some modifications dictated by requirements of technique or social conformity. Its potentialities are far more closely connected with those of photography and electrical sound developments. These media, however, have evolved entirely outside the domain of aesthetics, and aesthetic principles in relation to them are so insubstantial that they need not even be challenged. The possible contribution of these fields to the aesthetics of the motion picture is about the same as that of the physical theory of contrasting colours to the art of painting, or that of overtones to music.

Hence caution is particularly advisable with regard to pseudo-aesthetic considerations in the functionalist style, such as were popular in Germany in the name of the principle of *Materialgerechtigkeit,* or adequacy to the given material. With regard to the most essential instrument in cinema music – the microphone – the experience of the radio showed long ago that the creation of compositions 'adequate' to the microphone led in practice to an unjustifiable oversimplification of musical language.

So-called adjustment to such supposedly objective material conditions fetters musical imagination, generally for the sake of that kind of popularity which is the main concern of the motion-picture industry. The postulate of adequacy to the material would make sense only if it referred to the musical material in the proper meaning of the term, namely, to the tones and their relationships, not to extraneous and relatively accidental recording techniques. A truly functional procedure would consist in adapting the microphone to the requirements of the music, not vice versa. Even in architecture, which is practised with a tangible material, the term 'functional' would not be applied to a structure that is adapted to the nature of the trucks and cranes that serve for transporting the building material, but rather to one that is adapted to the nature of the available building material and the end of the whole. The microphone is a means of communication, not of construction. Incidentally, the progress of recording techniques has today made speculations on aesthetic limitations of that sort obsolete.

Even more dubious are speculations that seek to develop laws from the abstract nature of the media as such, for instance from the relation between optical and phonetical data in terms of the psychology of perception. At best this results in the ornamental applied-art duplicate of the 'abstract' picture. The antidote to commercialism in motion pictures is not the foundation of sects which dwell, let us say, on the affinity between certain colours and sounds and which mistake their obsessions for *avant-garde* ideas. Arbitrarily established rules for playing with the kaleidoscope are not criteria of art. If artistic beauty is derived exclusively from the material of the given art, it is degraded to the level of nature, but does not thereby acquire natural beauty. An art that aims at the geometrical purity, perfect proportions, and regularity of natural objects infects beautiful forms, if they are still beautiful at all, with the reflexive element that inevitably dissolves natural beauty. For the latter, 'both with regard to the abstract unity of form and the simplicity and purity of the sensuous material' is 'lifeless in its abstraction and is not a truly real unity. For true unity presupposes spiritual subjectivity, and this element is totally absent from natural beauty.'[1]

Basic Relation between the Music and the Picture

Thus far, Sergei Eisenstein has been the only important cinema director to enter into aesthetic discussions. He, too, polemizes against formalistic speculations about the relation between music and motion pictures, let alone between music and color. 'We conclude,' he writes,[2] 'that the existence of 'absolute' sound-color equivalents – even if found in nature – cannot play a decisive role in creative work, except in an occasional ''supplementary'' way.'

Such 'absolute equivalents' are, for instance, those between certain keys or chords and colors, of which the mirage has haunted theorists since Berlioz. Some of them are obsessed by the idea of associating every shade of color in a picture with an 'identical' sound. Even if such an identity existed – and it does not exist – and even if the method were not so atomistic that it flagrantly negates any continuity of artistic intent, the purpose of this identity would still be questionable. Why should one and the same thing be reproduced by two different media? The effect achieved by such repetition would be weaker rather than stronger.

Eisenstein also rejects the search for equivalents of 'the purely representational elements in music,' that is to say, the effort to achieve unity between picture and music by the addition of pictorial equivalents to the expressive associations of single musical themes or whole pieces.

However, Eisenstein himself is not altogether free from the formalistic type of thinking he so properly attacks. He inveighs against the shallowness of pictures based on a narrow representational idea of music; thus, the Barcarolle from *Tales of Hoffmann* inspired one film director to show a pair of lovers embracing against a background of Venetian scenery. 'But take from Venetian "scenes," ' he writes, 'only the approaching and receding movements of the water combined with the reflected scampering and retreating play of light over the surface of the canals, and you immediately remove yourself, by at least one degree, from the series of "illustration" fragments, and you are closer to finding a response to the sensed inner movement of a Barcarolle.' [3]

Such a procedure does not transcend the faulty principle of relating picture and music either by pseudo-identity or by association; it merely transfers the principle to a more abstract level, on which its crudeness and redundant character are less obvious. To reduce the visible waves to the mere motion of water and the play of light upon it, which is supposed to coincide with the undular character of the music, is to move toward the same kind of 'absolute equivalence' that Eisenstein rejects. It owes its absoluteness merely to the absence of any concrete limiting element.

The basic law formulated by Eisenstein reads: 'We must know how to grasp the movement of a given piece of music, locating its path (its line or form) as our foundation for the plastic composition that is to correspond to the music.'[4] The manner of thinking exemplified here is still formalistic, both too narrow and too vague. The basic concept of movement is ambiguous in both media. In music movement primarily signifies the underlying constant time unit, as it is approximately indicated by the metronome, although it may suggest something different; for instance, the smallest groups of notes (such as the semiquavers in a piece of the *Bumble Bee* type, the basic unit of which is, however, the crotchet). Or 'movement' is used in a higher sense, that of the so-called *Grossrhythmus,* the proportion between the parts and their dynamic relationship, the progression or the stopping of the whole, the breath pattern, so to speak, of the total form.

The concept of movement as it is used in motion pictures is even more ambiguous. It can mean the tangible and measurable rhythm of symmetrical optical structures, such as animated cartoons or ballets. If, in the name of higher unity, picture and music were made to present this rhythm incessantly and simultaneously, the relations between the two media would be pedantically restricted, and the result would be unbearable monotony. Movement can also mean a higher aesthetic quality of the motion picture; and it is this quality that Eisenstein obviously has in mind. Kurt London, too, introduces it under the name of 'rhythm,' declaring that it is 'derived from the various elements in its dramatic composition, and on the rhythm again is based the articulation of the style as a whole.'[5]

Such a 'rhythm' unquestionably does exist in the film, although a discussion of it can easily degenerate into empty phraseology. This rhythm results from the structure and proportions of the formal elements – as in musical compositions. To mention only two such 'higher' principles of movement, there are in the motion picture drama-like forms, i.e., extensive dialogues that employ the dramatic technique, with relatively few camera changes; and epic-like forms, i.e., sequences of short scenes, 'episodes' that are connected only through their content and meaning, frequently strongly contrasting with each other, without unity of space, time or main action. *The Little Foxes* is an instance of the dramatic form, and *Citizen Kane* of the epic form. But this rhythmical structure of the motion picture is neither necessarily complementary nor parallel to its musical structure. It might enter the process of composition, e.g., by the choice of short 'episodic' or long and elaborate musical forms, but this relationship would of necessity be of a very indirect and vague nature. Even the idea of adjusting the total structure of the music to that of the picture remains problematic, if for no deeper reason, because the music does not accompany the whole picture, and therefore cannot follow its temporal totality. One may admit that an ultimate relation between visual and musical form can be established, the common denominator being the 'sequence.' As long, however, as one remains on the level of generalities about movement or 'rhythm,' and looks for an accord of the two structures, the actual result is likely to be an affinity of moods – in other words, something suspiciously trite that contradicts the very principle of adequacy to the motion picture in the name of which that 'rhythm' or 'higher movement' is invoked. It is hardly an exaggeration to state that the concept of mood is altogether unsuitable to the motion picture as well as to advanced music. It is no accident that pictures supposed to express music usually resemble photographed landscapes or genre paintings, and strike one as spurious and stilted. And one cannot imagine Schönberg or Stravinsky stooping to compose genre music.

It is true that there must be some meaningful relation between the picture and the music. If silences, blank moments, tense seconds, are filled out with indifferent or naively heterogenous music, the result is a complete nuisance. Picture and music, however indirectly or even antithetically, must correspond to each other. It is a fundamental postulate that the specific nature of the picture sequence shall determine the specific nature of the accompanying music or that the specific music shall determine the specific sequence, although this latter case is today largely hypothetical. The actual inventive task of the composer is to compose music that 'fits' precisely into the given picture; intrinsic unrelatedness is here the cardinal sin. Even in marginal cases – for instance, when the scene of a murder in a horror picture is accompanied by deliberately unconcerned music – the unrelatedness of the accompaniment must be justified by the meaning of the whole as a special kind of relationship. Structural unity must be preserved even when the music is used as a contrast; the articulation of the musical accompaniment will usually correspond to the articulation of the motion-picture sequence, even when musical and pictorial expressions are diametrically opposed.

However, the unity of the two media is achieved indirectly; it does not consist in the identity between any elements, be it that between tone and colour or that of the 'rhythms' as a whole. The meaning or function of the elements is intermediary; they never coincide *per se*. If the concept of montage, so emphatically advocated by Eisenstein, has any justification, it is to be found in the relation between the picture and the music. From the aesthetic point of view, this relation is not one of similarity, but, as a rule, one of question and answer, affirmation and negation, appearance and essence. This is dictated by the divergence of the media in question and the specific nature of each. Music, however well defined in terms of its own structure, is never sharply defined with regard to any object outside itself to which it is related by imitation or expression. Conversely, no picture, not even an abstract painting, is completely emancipated from the world of objects.

The fact that it is the eye, not the ear, that perceives the world of objects affects even the freest artistic process: on the one hand, even the purely geometric figures of abstract painting appear like broken-off fragments of the visible reality; on the other hand, even the most crudely illustrative program music is at most related to this reality as a dream is to awakened consciousness. The facetiousness characteristic of all program music that does not naively attempt something that is impossible to it derives from that very circumstance: it manifests the contradiction between the reflected world of objects and the musical medium, and exploits this contradiction in order to enhance the effect of the music. Roughly speaking, all music, including the most 'objective' and non-expressive, belongs primarily to the sphere of subjective inwardness, whereas even the most spiritualized painting is heavily burdened with unresolved objectivity. Motion-picture music, being at the mercy of this relationship, should attempt to make it productive, rather than to negate it in confused identifications.

Montage

The application of the principle of montage to motion-picture music would help to make it more adequate to the present development phase, to begin with, simply because those media have been evolved independently of each other, and the modern technique by which they are brought together was not generated by them, but by the emergence of new facilities for reproduction. Montage makes the best of the aesthetically accidental form of the sound picture by transforming an entirely extraneous relation into a virtual element of expression.[6]

The direct merging of two media of such different historical origins would not make much more sense than the idiotic movie scripts in which a singer loses his voice and then regains it in order to supply a pretext for exhausting all the possibilities of photographed sound. Such a synthesis would limit motion pictures to those accidental cases in which both media somehow coincide, that is to say, to the domain of synaesthesia, the magic of moods, semi-darkness, and intoxication. In brief, the cinema would be confined to those expressive contents which, as Walter Benjamin showed, are basically incompatible with technical reproduction. The effects in which picture and music can be directly united are inevitably of the type that Benjamin calls 'auratic'[7] – actually they are degenerated forms of the 'aura,' in which the spell of the here and now is technically manipulated.

There can be no greater error than producing pictures of which the aesthetic ideas are incompatible with their technical premises, and which at the same time camouflage this incompatibility. In the words of Benjamin,

> It is noteworthy that even today particularly reactionary writers pursue the same line of thought, and see as the chief significance of motion pictures their capacity for expressing, if not the ritual, at least the supernatural elements of life. Thus, in discussing Reinhardt's production, *Midsummer Night's Dream*, Werfel says that it is doubtless the sterile imitation of the external world with its streets, interiors, railway station restaurants, cars and beaches, that has so far stood in the way of the rise of the motion picture to the realm of art. 'The motion picture,' to quote his words, 'has not yet grasped its true significance, its real potentialities ... These consist in its unique capacity for expressing the realm of the fairy tale, the miraculous and the supernatural with natural means and incomparable convincing power.' [8]

Such magical pictures would be characterized by the tendency to fuse the music and the picture and to avoid montage as an instrument for the cognition of reality. It is hardly necessary to stress the artistic and social implication of Werfel's program – pseudo-individualization achieved by industrial mass production.[9] It would also mark a retrogression from the achievements of modern music, which has freed itself from the *Musikdrama*, the programmatic school, and synaesthesia, and is working with might and main at the dialectical task of becoming unromantic while preserving its character of music. The sound picture without montage would amount to a 'selling out' of Richard Wagner's idea – and his work falls to pieces even in its original form.

Aesthetic models of genuine motion-picture music are to be found in the incidental music written for dramas or the topical songs and production numbers in musical comedies. These may be of little musical merit, but they have never served to create the illusion of a unity of the two media or to camouflage the illusionary character of the whole, but functioned as stimulants because they were foreign elements, which interrupted the dramatic context, or tended to raise this context from the realm of literal immediacy into that of meaning. They have never helped the spectator to identify himself with the heroes of the drama, and have been an obstacle to any form of aesthetic empathy.

It has been pointed out above that today's cultural industry unwittingly carries out the verdict that is objectively pronounced by the development of the art forms and materials. Applying this law to the relation between pictures, words, and music in the films, we might say that the insurmountable heterogeneity of these media furthers from the outside the liquidation of romanticism which is an intrinsic historical tendency within each art. The alienation of the media from each other reflects a society alienated from itself, men whose functions are severed from each other even within each individual. Therefore the aesthetic divergence of the media is potentially a legitimate means of expression, not merely a regrettable deficiency that has to be concealed as well as possible. And this is perhaps the fundamental reason why many light-entertainment pictures that fall far below the pretentious standards of the usual movie seem to be more substantial than motion pictures that flirt with real art. Movie revues usually come closest to the ideal of montage, hence music fulfils its proper function most adequately in them. Their potentialities are wasted only because of their standardization, their spurious romanticism, and their stupidly super-imposed plots of success-ful careers. They may be remembered if the motion picture is ever emancipated from the present-day conventions.

However, the principle of montage is suggested not merely by the intrinsic relation between pictures and music and the historical situation of the mechanically reproduced work of art. This principle is probably implied in the need that originally brought pictures and music together and that was of an antithetic character. Since their beginning, motion pictures have been accompanied by music. The pure cinema must have had a ghostly effect like that of the shadow play – shadows and ghosts have always been associated. The magic function of music that has been hinted at above probably consisted in appeasing the evil spirits uncon-sciously dreaded. Music was introduced as a kind of antidote against the picture. The need was felt to spare the spectator the unpleasantness involved in seeing effigies of living, acting, and even speaking persons, who were at the same time silent. The fact that they are living and nonliving at the same time is what constitutes their ghostly character, and music was introduced not to supply them with the life they lacked – this became its aim only in the era of total ideological planning – but to exorcise fear or help the spectator absorb the shock.[10]

Motion-picture music corresponds to the whistling or singing child in the dark. The real reason for the fear is not even that these people whose silent effigies are moving in front of one seem to be ghosts. The captions do their best to come to the aid of these images. But confronted with gesticulating masks, people experience themselves as creatures of the very same kind, as being threatened by muteness. The origin of motion-picture music is inseparably connected with the decay of spoken language, which has been demonstrated by Karl Kraus. It is hardly accidental that the early motion pictures did not resort to the seemingly most natural device of accompanying the pictures by dialogues of concealed actors, as is done in the Punch and Judy shows, but always resorted to music, although in the old horror or slapstick pictures it had hardly any relation to the plots.

The sound pictures have changed this original function of music less than might be imagined. *For the talking picture, too, is mute.* The characters in it are not speaking people but speaking effigies, endowed with all the features of the pictorial, the photographic two-dimensionality, the lack of spatial depth. Their bodiless mouths utter words in a way that must seem disquieting to anyone uninformed. Although the sound of these words is sufficiently different from the sound of natural words, they are far from providing 'images of voices' in the same sense in which photography provides us with images of people.

This technical disparity between picture and word is further accented by something much more deep-lying – the fact that all speech in motion pictures has an artificial, impersonal character. The fundamental principle of the motion picture, its basic invention, is the photographing of motions. This principle is so all-pervading that everything that is not resolved into visual motion has a rigid and heterogeneous effect with regard to the inherent law of the motion-picture form. Every movie director is familiar with the dangers of filmed theater dialogues; and the technical inadequacy of psychological motion pictures partly derives from their inability to free themselves from the dominance of the dialogue. By its material, the cinema is essentially related to the ballet and the pantomime; speech, which presupposes man as a self, rather than the primacy of the gesture, ultimately is only loosely superimposed upon the characters.

Speech in motion pictures is the legitimate heir to the captions; it is a roll retranslated into acoustics, and that is what it sounds like even if the formulation of the words is not bookish but rather feigns the 'natural.' The fundamental divergencies between words and pictures are uncon-sciously registered by the spectator, and the obtrusive unity of the sound picture that is presented as a complete reduplication of the external world with all its elements is perceived as fraudulent and fragile. Speech in the motion picture is a stop-gap, not unlike wrongly employed music that aims at being identical with the events on the screen. A talking picture without music is not very different from a silent picture, and there is even reason to believe that the more closely pictures and words are co-ordinated, the more emphatically their intrinsic contradiction and the actual muteness of those who seem to be speaking are felt by the spectators. This may explain – although the requirements of the market supply a more obvious reason – why the sound pictures still need music, while they seem to have all the opportunities of the stage and much greater mobility at their disposal.

Eisenstein's theory regarding movement can be appraised in the light of the foregoing discussion. The concrete factor of unity of music and pictures consists in the gestural element. This does not refer to the movement or 'rhythm' of the motion picture as such, but to the photographed motions and their function in the picture as a whole. The function of music, however, is not to 'express' this movement – here Eisenstein commits an error under the influence of Wagnerian ideas about the *Gesamtkunstwerk* and the theory of aesthetic empathy – but to release, or more accurately, to justify movement. The photographed picture as such lacks motivation for movement; only indirectly do we realize that the pictures are in motion, that the frozen replica of external reality has suddenly been endowed with the spontaneity that it was deprived of by its fixation, and that something petrified is manifesting a kind of life of its own. At this point music intervenes, supplying momentum, muscular energy, a sense of corporeity, as it were. Its aesthetic effect is that of a stimulus of motion, not a reduplication of motion. In the same way, good ballet music, for instance Stravinsky's, does not express the feelings of the dancers and does not aim at any identity with them, but only summons them to dance. Thus, the relation between music and pictures is antithetic at the very moment when the deepest unity is achieved.

The development of cinema music will be measured by the extent to which it is able to make this antithetic relation fruitful and to dispel the illusion of direct unity. The examples in the chapter on dramaturgy were discussed in reference to this idea. As a matter of principle, the relation between the two media should be made much more mobile than it has been. This means, on the one hand, that standard cues for interpolating music – as for background effect, or in scenes of suspense or high emotion

– should be avoided as far as possible and that music should no longer intervene automatically at certain moments as though obeying a cue. On the other hand, methods that take into account the relation between the two media should be developed, just as methods have been developed that take into account the modifications of photographic exposures and camera installations. Thanks to them, it would be possible to make music perceptible on different levels, more or less distant, as a figure or a background, over-distinct or quite vague. Even musical complexes as such might be articulated into their different sound elements by means of an appropriate recording technique.

Furthermore it should be possible to introduce music at certain points without any pictures or words, and at other points, instead of gradually concluding the music or cautiously fading it out, to break it off abruptly, for instance at a change of scenery. The true muteness of the talking picture would thus be revealed and would have to become an element of expression. Or the picture might be treated as a musical theme, to which the actual music would serve as a mere accompaniment, consisting of musical base figures without any leading voice.

Conversely, music might be used to 'out-shout' the action on the screen, and thus achieve the very opposite of what is demanded by conventional lyricism. This latter possibility was effectively exploited in the orchestrion scene of *Algiers,* where the noise of the mechanical instrument deafened the cries of mortal fear. However, even here the principle of montage was not fully applied, and the old prejudice that the music must be justified by the plot was respected.

The Problem of Style and Planning

The foregoing analyses have certain implications regarding the style of motion-picture music. The concept of style applies primarily to the unbroken unity of the organic work of art. Since the motion picture is not such a work of art and since music neither can nor should be part of such an organic unity, the attempt to impose a stylistic ideal on cinema music is absurd. We have sufficiently stressed the fact that the prevailing would-be romantic style is inadequate and spurious. If it were replaced by a radically 'functional' style, as might be the temptation in view of the technical character of the motion picture, and exclusively mechanical music were employed in the neoclassical manner, the result would be hardly more desirable. The present shortcomings – pseudo-psychological aesthetic empathy and redundant reduplication – would only give way to the defect of irrelevance. Nor can it be expected that a compromise, the middle course between the extremes, a style both expressive and constructivist, would remedy the evil. The piling up of antagonistic principles intended to safeguard the composition from all sides only defeats its purpose and in practice results in the achievement of old effects by new means. A hair-raising, 'thrilling' accompaniment to a murder scene will be essentially the same even if the whole tone scale is replaced with sharp dissonances.

Mere will to style is of no avail. What is needed is musical *planning*, the free and conscious utilization of all musical resources on the basis of accurate insight into the dramatic function of music, which is different in each concrete case. Such conscious and technically adequate musical planning has been attempted only in a few very exceptional instances. But it must be stated at once that even if the routine business obstacles were overcome, this type of planning would still have to cope with great objective difficulties. The tendency toward planning was inherent in the evolution of music itself, and it led to the ever greater control of the autonomous composer over his material. But under the conditions of the commercial cinema industry this tendency has many unfavorable aspects. By planning, the autonomous composer has emancipated himself from the dilettantism of so-called inspiration. He rules as a sovereign over his own imagination; it was said long ago that in every domain the genuine artist must master his spontaneous ideas. This is possible if the whole conception of the work is rooted in his freedom, is truly his own, and is not imposed upon him by another agency. His arbitrary rule is legitimate only in so far as the conception of the work, which is the goal of his efforts, preserves a non-arbitrary, purely expressive element. In the moving picture, the situation is quite different. The work, the goal, is determined extrinsically to a much greater extent than even by the text of the traditional opera. As a result, the arbitrary element is deprived of that sap of non-arbitrariness in the productive process, which raises what has been made to the level of something more than just 'having been made.' The achievements connected with the mastery of the material easily degenerate into calculated tricks, and the spontaneous element – which is indispensable, even though its value as an isolated quality is dubious – threatens to shrink. The progress of subjective mastery over the musical material jeopardizes the subject expressing himself musically.

Moreover, conscious selection among possibilities instead of abiding by a 'style' might lead to syncretism, the eclectic utilization of all conceivable materials, procedures, and forms. It may produce indiscriminately love songs composed in terms of romantic expressiveness, callously functional accompaniments of scenes that are intended to be disavowed by the music, and the mode of expressionism in scenes to which music is supposed to supply tempestuous outbreaks. Such dangers make themselves felt in today's muddling-through practice. It is only a special instance of the general practice of rummaging through all our cultural inheritance for commercial purposes which characterizes the cultural industry.

An effective way to meet that danger can be formulated on the basis of a closer scrutiny of the concept of style. When the question of an adequate style for motion-picture music is raised, one usually has in mind the musical resources of a specific historical phase. Thus impressionism is identified with the whole-tone scale, chords on the ninth and shifting harmonies; romanticism suggests the most conspicuous formulas of composers like Wagner and Tchaikovsky; functionalism is conceived as the sum total of 'drained' harmonies, rudely stamping movements, pre-classical *head* motifs, terrace-like forms, and certain patterns that can be found in Stravinsky and to some extent in Hindemith.

Such an idea of style is incompatible with motion-picture music, which can employ resources of the most varied character. What counts is the way these resources are handled. Of course, the two elements, the resources and their treatment, cannot be mechanically separated. Debussy's procedure is the consequence of the inherent necessities of his musical material, and, vice versa, this material is derived from his method of composing. However, one may venture the thesis that today music has reached a phase in which its resources and methods of composing are becoming increasingly independent of each other. As a result, the material tends to be in some aspects rather irrelevant to the method of composing.

In other words, composing has become so logical that it need no longer be the consequence of its material and can, figuratively speaking, dominate every type of material to which it is applied. It is not accidental that Schönberg, after evolving the twelve-tone technique and achieving complete and consistent command of his material in all its dimensions, tested his mastery on a piece consisting only of triads, such as the last choir of opus 36, or that he added the finale of the Second Chamber Symphony. This finale, written forty years after the symphony had been conceived, brings to the fore the constructive principles of the twelve-tone technique within musical material that represents the stage of development of about forty years ago. Of course, such a feat represents only a tendency, and is inseparable from Schönberg's incomparable productive power.

As a matter of principle, priority goes to the truly novel musical resources. However, motion-picture music can also summon other musical resources of the most varied nature, on condition that it reaches the most advanced contemporary modes of composing, which are characterized by thorough-going construction and the unequivocal determination of each detail by the whole, and which are thus in line with the principle of universal planning, so fundamental for motion-picture music. Thus the negation of the traditional concept of style, which is bound up with the idea of specific materials, may lead to the formation of a new style suitable to the movies.

It goes without saying that such a style is not yet achieved when a composer is only shrewd enough to accompany a sequence with some material that happens to fit. One would be justified in speaking of a new style only if the disposal of such arbitrarily selected material reflected the most highly developed experience of modern composing. If this experience is truly present, the composer may also use triads; when subjected to the principle of construction they will sound so strange in any event that they will have nothing in common with the lyrical ripple of the late-romantic convention and will strike the conventional ear as dissonance. In other words, obsolete musical material, if it is really put to use and not just commercialized by the motion picture, will undergo, by the application of the principle of construction, a refraction relating both to its expressive content and its purely musical essence. Occasionally, musical planning may provide for applying the principle of montage to the music itself, that is to say, it may employ contradictory stylistic elements without mediation, and exploit their very inconsistency as an artistic element.

In all this, one must not overlook the situation of the composer himself. It would be vain to decree 'objectively' what is timely or not, while dodging the question whether the composer is capable of doing what the times seem to require. For he is not merely an executive organ of knowledge, a mirror of necessities outside himself; he represents the element of spontaneity, and cannot be divested of his subjectivity in any of his objective manifestations. Any musical planning that ignored this would degenerate into arbitrary mechanical rules.

This does not refer merely to the fact that many composers, and not necessarily the worst ones, lag behind the intellectual level of planning procedures in their method of composing; theory cannot condemn even them as unfit for writing motion-picture music. But the situation of any motion-picture composer, including the most modern one, is to some extent self-contradictory. His task is to aim at certain sharply defined musical profiles relating to plots and situations, and to transform them into musical structures; and he must do this much more drastically and with much more objective aloofness than was ever required in the older forms of musical drama. At the end of the era of expressive music, it is the principle of *musica ficta* that triumphs – the postulate that it must represent something to which it refers instead of merely being itself. This alone is paradoxical enough and involves the greatest difficulties. The composer is supposed to express something, be it even by way of negating expression, but not to express himself; and whether' this can be done by a music that has emancipated itself from all traditional patterns of expression is impossible to decide beforehand.

The composer is confronted with a veritable task of Sisyphus. 'He is supposed to abstract himself from his own expressive needs and to abide by the objective requirements of dramatic and musical planning. But he can achieve this only in so far as his own subjective possibilities and even his own subjective urges can assimilate those requirements and gratify them spontaneously – anything else would be mere drudgery. Thus the subjective prerequisite of the composer's work is the very element that the supposed objectivity of this work excludes; he must, so to speak, both be and not be the subject of his music. Whether this contradiction will lead we cannot predict at the present stage of development, when it has not even been visualized by normal production. But it can be observed that certain apparently sophisticated, aloof, and objective solutions that sacrifice the expressive urges to avoid the romanticist jargon, e.g., some French cinema composers in the orbit of the Circle of the Six, result in a tendency toward automatism and boring applied-art mannerisms.

Not only theoretical reflection but also technological experience raises the question of style. All motion-picture music has so far displayed a tendency to neutralization[11] – there is almost always an element of inconspicuousness, weakness, excessive adaptation, and familiarity in it. Frequently enough it does exactly what it is supposed to do according to the current prejudice, that is to say, it vanishes and remains unnoticed by the spectator who is not especially interested in it.[12] The reasons for this are complex. First of all there is the system of cultural industry with its standardization, and countless conscious and unconscious mechanisms of censorship, which result in a general levelling process, so that every single incident becomes a mere specimen of the system, and its apprehension as something specific is practically impossible. This, however, affects both pictures and music, and explains the general inattention in the perception of movies, correlated to the relaxation that they supposedly serve, rather than the fact that the music is not noticed. This latter circumstance is the result of the spectators' concentration on the visual plot and the dialogue, which leaves him little energy for musical perception. The physiological effort necessarily connected with the act of following a motion picture plays a primary role in this context.

Apart from that, however, the existing recording procedures are themselves responsible for neutralization. Motion-picture music, like radio music, has the character of a running thread – it seems to be drawn along the screen before the spectator, it is more a picture of music than music itself. At the same time it undergoes far-reaching acoustic changes, its dynamic scale shrinks, its color intensity is reduced, and its spatial depth is lost. All these changes converge in their effects; if one is present at the recording of an advanced cinema score, then listens to the sound tracks, and finally attends the performance of the picture with its 'printed' music, the progressive grades of neutralization can be observed. It is as though the music were gradually divested of its aggressiveness, and in the final performance the question whether the score is modern or old-fashioned has far less importance than one might expect from merely reading it or even from listening to the same music in the concert hall. Even conservative listeners in the cinema swallow without protest music that in a concert hall would arouse their most hostile reactions.

In other words, as a result of neutralization, musical style in the usual sense, that is to say, the resources employed in each case, becomes largely indifferent. For this reason, the aim of a genuine montage and an antithetic utilization of music will not be to introduce the largest possible number of dissonant sounds and novel colors into the machinery, which only spits them out again in a digested, blunted, and conventionalized form, but to break the mechanism of neutralization itself.[13] And that is the very function of planned composition. Of course, there may always be situations that require inconspicuous music, as a mere background. But it makes all the difference in the world whether such situations are part of the plan and whether the inconspicuousness of the music is composed and constructed, or whether the expulsion of music into the acoustic and aesthetic background is the result of blind, automatic compulsion. Indeed, a genuine background effect can be obtained only by planning, not as a result of mechanical absence of articulation. The difference between the two kinds of effects can be likened to that between Debussy, who most perfectly and distinctly created a vague, indistinct, and dissolving impression, and some blunderer who extols his own involuntarily vague, amorphous, and confused structure, the product of an insufficient technique as the embodiment of an aesthetic principle.

Objective planning, montage, and breaking through the universal neutralization are all aspects of the emancipation of motion-picture music from its commercial oppression. The social need for a non-predigested, uncensored, and critical function of music is in line with the inherent technological tendency to eliminate the neutralization factors. Objectively planned music, organically constructed in relation to the meaning of the picture, would, for the first time, make the potentialities of the new improved recording techniques productive.

Insight into the contradictions characteristic of the relations between motion pictures and music shows that there can be no question of setting up universal aesthetic criteria for this music. It is superfluous and harmful, says Hegel, 'to bring one's yardsticks and apply one's personal intuitions and ideas to the inquiry; it is only by omitting these that we are enabled to examine the subject matter as it is in and for itself.'[13] The application of this principle does not surrender motion-picture music to arbitrariness; it means that the criteria of this music must be derived in each given case from the nature of the problems it raises. The task of aesthetic considerations is to throw light on the nature of these problems and their requirements, to make us aware of their own inherent development, not to provide recipes.

6
The Composer and the Movie-Making Process

It is beyond the scope of this book to give a description of the processing to which the score of a motion-picture composition is subjected. This processing includes recording, cutting, re-recording and final modifications related to the picture as a whole. It involves numerous purely technological factors that have little to do with the dramatic and aesthetic aspects of the question, and that the composer does not have to understand any more than the author of a book needs to understand the art of printing. Moreover, the relevant technological factors vary to a considerable extent.

Yet the analogy between the making of a picture and the printing of a book must not be carried too far. As regards content and literary value, a book remains substantially, although not completely, the same regardless of how it is printed. But there is no such thing as a motion picture independent of technical recording processes. The manuscript of a book is actually the book itself; a motion-picture script at best consists of the directions for the creation of the picture. This is the basis for the following discussion in which we shall deal with artistic aspects of the process of production, indicate the musical nerve centres of the film industry, and emphasize elements essential in motion-picture composing. We shall try to communicate actual experiences, not to evolve a theory regarding the musical technique of motion pictures. The fact that in these considerations the technical problems of composing are in the foreground is a corollary of the point of view chosen for this book as a whole. Furthermore, the composer will be reminded at which points he must proceed with care if he does not wish to be intimidated by certain compulsory elements of the productive process, which he often does not understand, capitulating to them rather than making them as fruitful as possible.

The Music Departments

Because of the commercial character of the film industry it is impossible to separate its organizational from its technical aspects, and the composer must acquaint himself, from the outset, with the prevailing organizational principles. As a result of the rigid division of functions within the great companies, where all the important positions have long since been occupied and controlled, there have been set up special music departments, which are responsible to the producers for the artistic, technical, and commercial aspects of motion-picture music, and which have thus assumed full authority with regard to the composers. The situation is different in the case of some independent producers; there the composer must content himself with relatively limited resources, but is also less restricted. But under average conditions, the composer is far from enjoying equal rights with the producer, script writer, or film director. He is subject to the head of the music department, who regards him as a kind of specialist. Like all specialists he is either employed under a long-term contract or hired for a specific job. Thus the composer is usually in a dependent position; he is only loosely connected with the enterprise and can be easily dismissed.

In view of the composition of the departments, which has been discussed in chapter 4, conflicts are almost inevitable. Music-department heads generally select composers according to their own taste, just as directors 'cast' their actors; only in exceptional cases are composers appointed by different agencies, and even then their situation is not always an easy one. In relation to the organization as a whole, the composer, however important he may be, occupies a subsidiary place; he must above all satisfy the department head who is his 'boss.' He is looked upon as one of the latter's assistants, like the arranger, the conductor or the sound man. The extent to which he succeeds in influencing the musical planning, performance, and recording procedure depends on his authority, adroitness, and, most important, the support he can obtain outside the department. It behoves him to face these conditions without any illusions and to approach his job in a manner that will enable him to accomplish as much as possible within the existing set-up. Up until now it has proved impossible to break through it and to put the composer on the same level as the script writer.

Nevertheless, the composer would be wrong to regard the department as his enemy *a priori,* and to begin his work in a rebellious mood. The role of the music departments reflects a much more general state of affairs. Despite the inadequacy, the often grotesque artistic incompetence of the heads, and the conceit prevailing in the departments, the technical and economic aspects of the film industry are so complex that without the organization and division of functions of which the department is an expression, nothing could be accomplished, at least under the prevailing conditions. The composer may feel that the department is nothing but a bureaucratic impediment and control agency for businessmen, but without it he would be completely lost in the machinery. The path from the score to the finished musical product, or the realization of artistic intentions, leads often across artistic incompetence and agencies dedicated to the business of making money. The departments are both superfluous and indispensable. They could be dispensed with if artistic production were emancipated from the profit motive; but today it is impossible to accomplish anything without their resources, mediating services, and often their experience. The composer must take this inevitable contradiction into consideration. While he should not be a conformist, he should not make a fool of himself either. Both attitudes would only manifest his impotence.

General Observations on Composing

The motion picture requires *prima facie* no specific technique of composing. The fact that both motion picture and music are temporal arts does not imply the need for a musical technique *sui generis,* and despite all talk about such a technique, the motion picture has not given a genuine new impulse to music. Motion-picture music has merely adapted certain procedures employed in autonomous music.

Nevertheless certain principles are beginning to take shape. One has been mentioned above – the need for short musical forms, corresponding to the short picture sequences. Such sketchy, rhapsodical, or aphoristic forms are characteristic of the motion picture in their irregularity, fluidity, and absence of repetitions. The traditional tripartite song form – *a-b-a* – with the last part repeating the first, is less suitable than continuous forms, such as preludes, inventions, or toccatas. The method of exposition and connection of several themes and their developments seems foreign to the motion picture because such complex musical forms require too much attention to be used in combination with complex visual forms. But even this is not an absolute rule. Large musical forms related not to picture sequences but to continuities of meaning are not inconceivable.

In short musical forms, each element must be self-sufficient or capable of rapid expansion. Motion-picture music cannot 'wait.' Moreover, the composer must differentiate among the short forms themselves. For instance, a two-minute sequence is more suitable for developing a short motif than for a complete melody, and a thirty-second theme would be out of place here. But this does not mean that in a thirty-second *piece* the theme must be still shorter; on the contrary, it may very well consist of one long melody that covers the whole sequence.

The specific musical logic that assigns each of these elements a definite place and connects them must also be adequate to the requirements of the motion picture. Quickly changing musical characterizations, sudden transitions and reversals, improvisatory and 'fantasia' elements should be predominant. To achieve this without sacrificing musical continuity one must resort to a highly evolved variation technique. Each small musical form accompanying a motion picture is a kind of variation, even though it has not been preceded by a manifest theme. The dramatic function is the real theme.

As has already been pointed out, the composer cannot disregard the planning that is demanded by the dramatic concern for the whole of the motion picture and its relation to the details. But while thus far planning has been bureaucratic and artistically barren, he must attempt to make it fruitful. He must consciously use the simple and the complex, the continuous and the discontinuous, the inconspicuous and the striking, the passionate and the cold elements of music. The free and conscious utilization of the potentialities created by the intrinsic evolution of music will make motion-picture music fertile, if a specific motion-picture music ever comes into being at all. Planning must be transformed to such an extent that it will amount to a new spontaneity. The negation of naive 'inventing' and inspiration in motion-picture music should lead to their re-emergence on a higher level.

We shall mention at least the simplest consequences of the type of composing advocated here. With regard to the logic and the genesis of the work, there are, grossly speaking, two types of composition. In the first, the whole is derived from the details, conceived as musical germs, and developed blindly under the compulsion of their inherent drive. The works of Schubert and Schumann belong to this type, and originally also those of Schönberg, who said that when composing a song he allowed himself to be impelled by the initial words without taking the whole poem into consideration. In the second type, which is the inverse of the first, all the details are derived from the whole. The works of Beethoven belong to the second type. The greatness of a composer is essentially defined by the extent to which both types are integrated in his work – Bach, Mozart, Beethoven, and Schönberg are exemplary in this respect. If the composer clings undialectically to the first type of composing, as did Dvořák for instance, he produces a potpourri of 'ideas' connected arbitrarily or schematically. The other extreme is represented by Handel, and leads to a sweeping though somewhat abstract conception of the whole, with sketchy, incomplete, and often superficial details.

Composers of cinema music are driven to adopt the second type of composing, as is, incidentally, the case for most works made to order. In motion-picture music, the idea of the whole and its articulation holds absolute primacy, sometimes in the form of an abstract pattern that conjures up rhythms, tone sequences, and figures at a given place without the composer's specific knowledge of them in advance. The composer must invent forms and formal relations, not 'ideas,' if he is to write meaningfully. He can master the resulting difficulties only by realizing them clearly and translating them into well-defined technical problems, by dividing his procedure rationally into different steps and ultimately achieve 'invention.' He must have a kind of blue-print in mind, a framework which he must fill in at each given place and only then see to it that the fillings are vivid and striking. In a sense, he must have full control over elements that in traditional composing are, often wrongly, considered to be involuntary and purely intuitive.

This filling in, this consummation of the concrete, is the Achilles' heel of composing for motion pictures. Since the filling in is planned, by its nature it threatens at every step to degenerate into mere padding, which will appear dry, synthetic, and mechanical if the composer fails to bring in sufficient spontaneity to counter the impact of his own plan. The result is then one of those peculiar compositions, which despite their mediocre musical substance have a certain effectiveness that derives from a felicitous idea of the whole. The current demand for showmanship on the part of the composer refers to this specific musical ability, the flair for the function, without demanding an equivalent sense of the material by which it is being fulfilled. Once the composer has reached the level of planned composing, be must focus his whole energy and critical judgment on the problem of filling in.

Regarding the thesis of the primacy of the whole, or form in a broad sense, in motion-picture music, it must be emphasized that the galaxy of forms evolved by traditional music and expounded in academic theories is largely useless. Many traditional forms must be discarded; others must be completely modified. To realize the primacy of the whole in motion-picture music thus does not mean to take over the forms of absolute music and to adapt them by hook or crook to the film strips – by analogy with certain tendencies of contemporary opera, for instance those of Berg and Hindemith – but the very opposite. It means building complete form structures according to the specific requirements of the given film sequence, and then 'filling in.' Good motion-picture music is fundamentally anti-formalistic. The inadequacy of traditional forms and the possibility of replacing them with advanced music has been discussed in a previous chapter, and the prosaic character of motion pictures and their general incompatibility with repetitions and musical symmetries have been defined as the most important factors in that inadequacy. We shall now discuss a number of other formal problems from the point of view of motion-picture requirements, disregarding the specific musical resources.

The prose quality of motion pictures cannot be taken into account by the mere omission of repetitions in their various forms, such as the 'a' part of the three-part song form, while in all other respects the composition follows the traditional pattern, for instance, that of the sonata exposition, which has been the prototype of all musical form for more than 150 years. In autonomous music there are a number of elements that have meaning only within the given formal set-up, in 'looking forward' or 'looking back' to some purely musical content. The recapitulation in the classical sonata, with its structural change of the modulation scheme that closes the circle of the form movement, is only the most tangible instance of this fact. But such elements are found even in the traditional exposition. The whole classical sonata form rests on the premise that not all musical moments are equally relevant as such – indeed, that not all of them are present to the same extent – but that the presence of musical events is more intense with entrance and re-entrance of the themes, and is meaningfully less intense in other passages. The very essence of the traditional sonata form is defined by the variable degree of presence of musical events, that is, their differentiation according to whether they are perceived 'themselves,' as anticipated or remembered, or only prepare for or lead away from such anticipations or recollections. Their articulation is equivalent to their different density or presence at different moments. Not the symphonic movement in which everything is equally present, or, to use technical terms, in which everything is equally thematic, is the best, but the symphonic movement in which the present and nonpresent moment are related in the deepest and most comprehensive manner.

Only in the latest stages of autonomous music, in such works as Schönberg's *Erwartung,* are all the musical elements equally near the centre. And even Schönberg, since he introduced the twelve-tone technique, seems to have been striving for differentiation according to the different degree of presence. Transitional parts, fields of tension, and fields of release of tension are some of the resources of this differentiation. It was just these elements of form which, in contrast to the 'inventions' or the actual themes, were most exposed to bad schematic treatment, but it was also through these same elements that the principle of the dynamic construction of the whole triumphantly asserted itself in great works, such as the *Eroica.* These elements, whose meaning consists in the unfolding of an autonomous musical continuity, are denied to the motion picture, which requires a thoroughly and completely present music, a music that is not self-contemplative, self-reflective, that does not harbour anticipations in itself. When transitions or fields of tension are needed, they come from the sequence of the picture, not from the inner movement of the music. This circumstance alone sets very narrow limits to the adoption of traditional patterns.

On the other hand, the composer is confronted with problems of form that hardly ever occurred in traditional music. For instance, a sequence can require the 'exposition' of an event, but it must be done with a concentrated brevity that was completely alien to the sonata exposition before the disintegration of tonality. Thus the composer must be able to write music of a preparatory character that is also entirely present and does not utilize the stale means for creating moods, such as the repulsive tremolo crescendi or other devices of the same kind. He must be able to compose concluding passages, which round up a preceding dramatic development of the picture or dialogue, without a preceding purely musical and closed development – something like a *stretta* without a preceding *più moderato.* The concluding character must be found in the structure of the music itself in the drastic characterization of its smallest components, not in their relation to preceding components, which do not exist in this case. Climaxes must sometimes be brought about directly, without crescendos, or only with a minimum of preparation.

This presents a considerable difficulty, for musically there is the greatest difference between a simple forte or fortissimo passage and one that has the effect of a climax. But while formerly a climax resulted from the whole development, here it must be achieved, so to speak, separately, 'in itself.' There is no general rule for such a procedure, but the composer must be aware of the problem. It may he said that such an 'absolute' climax without preceding intensification can be achieved through the nature and emphasis of the musical profiles themselves, not through the mere impact of noise. Every musician knows that there are themes with an inherent 'concluding' character, which is difficult to describe in words, but is accessible to careful analysis. The closing section of the exposition of the first movement of the Pastoral Symphony, the brief closing theme in the first movement of piano sonata op. 101, or bars 82 and following in the larghetto of the Second Symphony are instances of such themes in Beethoven. Likewise there are 'primary' and 'auxiliary' characterizations as such. The composer of motion-picture music must be aware of such qualities in his material and attempt to produce them directly, without the detour of preparation and resolution. The effects in question require nothing that is alien to music. They have largely crystallized inside the shell of the traditional form language. But the point is to give them new validity by conceiving them as an independent result of that form language. It is necessary to emancipate them from their usual formal presuppositions that are incompatible with the cinema, to make them fluid, as it were.

Non-schematic forms are also known in traditional music under the name of fantasies and rhapsodies. While the latter often approximate the potpourri or, like Brahms' opus 79 and, to some extent, Schubert's *Wanderer Fantasy,* are disguised song forms or sonatas, there is such a thing as a specific fantasy form, such as Mozart's famous piano fantasies in C-minor and D-minor. Official musical theory has kept aloof from such works and contented itself with declaring that they had no definite form. Yet Mozart's two fantasies mentioned above are no less carefully organized than the sonatas, indeed, perhaps even more carefully, because they are not subjected to a heteronomous order. Their formal principle might be termed that of the segment, or the 'intonation.' They consist of a number of parts, each of them unified, relatively complete, each following a single thematic pattern, in different tempos and keys. The art of the fantasy consists not so much in elaboration and development of a uniformly flowing totality as in balancing the various segments through similarity and contrast, careful proportions,[1] modulated characterizations, and a certain looseness of structure. The segments may often be suddenly interrupted. The less definite their form, the more easily can they be joined to others and continued by them. All this is similar to the requirements of motion-picture music. Its composer will often be compelled to think in terms of segments rather than of developments, and what is accomplished elsewhere by the form resulting from the thematic development, he will have to achieve by relating one segment to another. This is a direct consequence of the postulate of 'presence' in motion-picture music, and refers to relatively large pieces, which for the time being are infrequent.

The interrelation of several forms also raises questions that cannot be solved by means of traditional resources alone. Contrast through tempo is insufficient. From a dramatic point of view it may be deemed necessary that several movements in the same tempo should follow one another, and that, as in the older suite, they should differ sharply, but only in character. For instance, a slow tempo was out of place in the newly composed music to Joris Ivens' *Rain*, not because it was necessary to illustrate the falling of the rain, but because the music's task was to push forward this plotless and therefore static motion picture. The composer was forced to adopt means of contrast more subtle than the allegro followed by an adagio. Thus motion-picture music does not necessarily lead to the use of coarser means; on the contrary, if it is emancipated, it will be a stimulus for new differentiations.

It must be kept in mind that the planning of the music can be effective only if it is not separated from the planning of the picture; the two aspects must be in productive interrelation. If the composer is faced with given sequences and told to contribute thirty seconds of music at one place and two minutes at another place, his planning is confined to the very bureaucratic function from which he should be freed. Such a planning is founded on the mechanical and administrative division of competence, not on the inherent conditions of the work. Free planning signifies combined planning, which could often lead to fitting the picture to the music, instead of the usual inverse procedure. This would of course presuppose genuine collective work in the motion-picture industry. Eisenstein seems to be working in this direction.

Music and Noise

Under conditions of responsible planning, well-arranged noise strips might in many cases be preferable to music. This is particularly true of background music with simultaneous dialogue. The role of a mere stage setting is incompatible with the nature of articulated, developed music and its adequate perception. Either it retains its character of music, and then it diverts the spectator's attention, or it tends spontaneously to approximate noise, and then the musical appearance becomes super-fluous. Of course, it is often necessary to mingle music and noise, because noise alone might produce an effect of dullness and emptiness. But in such cases noise and music must be mutually adjusted. In terms of music, this means that it has to 'keep open' for the noise, which is to be integrated into it. The function of noise is twofold: on the one hand, it is naturalistic, and on the other, it is an element of the music itself, with an effect that can best be likened to the accents of the percussion instruments.

From the foregoing it can be inferred: (1) that the rhythmic beats of noise are provided for in the music, which, so to speak, reserves a place for it; and (2) that the tone colour of the music is either similar to that of the noise or is deliberately and distinctly contrasted with it. For example, a man flees from danger in a bustling street and reaches a door. The ringing of the bell concludes rapid string figures in the manner of a cadenza. Thus music can dissolve into noises, or noises can dissolve into music, as though they were dissonances.

Occasionally noise and music can be planned in co-ordination for a long sequence. For instance, the screen shows a view of roofs in a city. All the bells of the city begin to ring while ever new masses of roofs and steeples are projected. A close-up shows the symbolic figure of death emerging from a clock mechanism and striking a bell with a hammer. At the end of the sequence a coffin is shown, while the dull echo of a church knell is still audible. The accompanying music is characterized by monumental coldness, and uses bells as an ingredient. But this is insufficient to produce the density of sound resulting from the full ringing of many bells, which is necessary for dramatic reasons. Such an effect cannot be achieved if the picture and music are recorded simultaneously, for the rhythmic irregularity of the bell sounds cannot be adapted to a conductor's beat. For that reason, in the example cited here, the sound had to be produced synthetically by combining several sound tracks: in addition to the music track, there were four separate tracks for the bells, and two more for the church knell and the hammer stroke of death. The four bell tracks were arranged to form a correlated whole. In the re-recording, all the tracks were combined with the music track, and various elements were alternately stressed. The point of this discussion is that effects of this kind cannot be left to chance. A satisfactory result was achieved in this instance only because the noise tracks had been produced with due consideration for the music and because the total effect had been carefully prepared.

Recording of noises has done away with program music. The musical reproduction of a storm cannot compete with the recording of a real storm. Tone painting has become strikingly superfluous – in fact it has always been. It is justified only if it achieves what Beethoven demanded of it in the Pastoral Symphony, i.e., 'the expression of feelings, rather than painting,' or if it adds emphasis, over-explicit light, so to speak, and tends to virtuosity, deliberately introducing artificiality, instead of striving for realistic effects. Attempts to outdo a real rain by a musical rain, or to invent the musical sound of a snowfall ('that is how falling snow should sound') may lead to delightful effects, but these, of course, have nothing in common with the traditional idea of program music.

Setting[2] Technique and Instrumentation

Concerning 'setting' technique and instrumentation – for a good composer both are identical – the first thing to be noted is that the postulate of suitability for the microphone, which was still fashionable in 1932, has since then become obsolete. The progress of music recording has made it possible to reproduce any score with reasonable adequacy. This was not always the case. Double and triple stops of string instruments, instruments of extreme range, such as the double bass and piccolo, and horns, flutes, and oboes, indeed the whole traditional string section, were more difficult to reproduce than other instruments and combinations of sounds. Today the sound-recording apparatus has been greatly improved. That also means, naturally, that a poorly orchestrated composition will sound as bad in recording as it sounded originally.

The limits of 'setting' and instrumentation are no longer set by the inadequacy of the recording apparatus, but by the dramatic function of the music. In concert music, a complex style such as Schönberg's is the result of a specific musical evolution. It would be legitimate in motion-picture music only if it corresponded to definite dramatic requirements. When music is driven toward the margin of the field of attention, as is the case in the motion picture, its perceptibility is narrowly restricted. It would be absurd to write more complex music than can actually be perceived at any given moment. Even the subtlest problems of musical setting depend upon the planning of the motion picture as a whole.

Today musical planning is achieved only in a distorted way as a result of the mechanical separation between the composition – 'setting' – and arrangement – 'instrumentation.' Such a planning is more of an industrial façade than a genuinely organized procedure, and cannot be justified either objectively or economically. This particular division of labour has a spurious character, it is based only on considerations of personnel. In reality, any qualified composer should be able to invent his instrumentation together with his music, instead of first composing and then orchestrating it. It takes no more time to compose a score than to reduce a still nonexistent orchestral version to a dubious piano score. Division of labor here leads to entrusting the composing proper to amateurs, who are thus encouraged to write, because their grossest errors are corrected by the arranger, while still other experts rule over the supposedly mysterious domain of orchestration, just as is the case in Tin Pan Alley. On the other hand, the emergence of specialized arrangers has led to the standardization of instrumentation itself. All this results in a tiresome uniformity of all motion-picture scores. Even the most talented arranger grows sterile through constant handling of poor material. However, this absurd procedure is almost inevitable under the present conditions in the industry. The composers often work under great pressure and have to produce enormous quantities of music – eighty minutes of accompaniment to a motion picture – so that they themselves are unable to do the considerable writing work required by a score, even when they imagine the instruments as vividly as possible in the course of composing. It is no accident that even among the highly qualified composers in Hollywood hardly anyone orchestrates his own works. Considering the relatively high standard of the arrangers, this does not seem too great a misfortune. In reality, however, the division of labor means that an important part of the work of composing is omitted. Any self-critical composer, when preparing the final score, retouches and corrects, he never transcribes mechanically. The use of arrangers eliminates this delicate part of instrumentation, because the arranger either faithfully follows the composer's original indications or, if such indications are lacking, replaces them with the safest and most oft-tried effects, whereas the composer himself might have found what was specifically needed in the given passage. Thus a further factor of leveling is introduced.

To some extent this sterility can also be attributed to the type of orchestras prevalent in today's studios. It is true that a good composer can achieve great variety even with the most modest instrumental resources. But certain standard restrictions in the disposition of the instruments nevertheless tend to standardize the sound itself. This refers above all to the pseudo-glamorous titles and endings, to the monotonous homophony always with blurred middle voices, to the predominance of honeyed violin tones, the undifferentiated treatment of woodwinds, among which only the bassoon stands out as the village clown and the oboe as the innocent lamb, and the ponderous brass chords. Aside from a kind of dialogue between the strings and the brasses, almost nothing can be heard except an obtrusive upper voice accompanied by a feeble bass.

The disposition of the string section is particularly absurd. With few exceptions, it consists of twelve to sixteen violins, treated usually as one voice (i.e., first and second violins in unison), two or three violas, two or three cellos, and two double basses. The disproportion between instruments of high and low range preclude any distinct polyphony in the strings and leads to the practice of 'laying it on' with mere stop-gap voices.

There is a similar disproportion between woods and brasses. Four horns, three trumpets, two or three trombones, and a tuba are often balanced by two flutes and, it must be granted, three clarinets (which usually duplicate the strings), one and rarely two oboes, alternating with the English horn, and often only one bassoon. The problem of an adequate wind bass has not been satisfactorily solved even in concert and opera orchestras; the studio orchestras ignore it. But even the higher woodwinds are generally used as padding or play in unison with the strings.

As a rule, full orchestras are employed only at the beginning and the end, and for particularly important sequences; all the rest – intimate music, background music for dialogues, accompaniments for short sequences – is supplied by a small orchestra, lacking almost all of the brasses and woodwinds, but retaining most of the strings. The result is music that sounds intolerably like that in a café. The harp and the piano, which are never absent, contribute their sugary coloration, mechanical distinctness, and spurious fullness.

If there must be both a large and a small orchestra, they should be better proportioned, and more drastically distinguished from each other, not only by the number, but also by the nature of their instruments. The complete orchestra should far more approximate the symphony orchestra than is the practice today, with a sufficient number of second violins, violas, cellos, and double basses, and with twice or three times as many woodwinds. This is done in isolated cases, but it should be the rule. On the other hand, the small orchestra should correspond to a genuine chamber ensemble – flutes, clarinets, solo violin, solo cello, and piano – or might consist of string quartet, flute, clarinet, and bassoon. Many such combinations could easily be formed; they have long since proved their extraordinary value for chamber music; the first one mentioned, for instance, is used by Schönberg in his *Pierrot Lunaire*. If new instruments are also included, such as the novachord, electric piano, electric guitar, electric violin, and others, and these are employed independently and not, as is usual today, for mere color effects and doubling. the way will be open for countless interesting possibilities, a real composer's paradise. The following two combinations have proved their worth: (1) clarinet, trumpet, novachord, electric piano, and guitar; and (2) novachord, electric piano, violin, and flute.

Lately there has appeared a tendency to relax the standardization of motion-picture orchestras by the introduction of unusual colors obtained, apart from the electric instruments, through the use of delicate woodwinds, such as the alto flute and the contrabass clarinet. It is well to remember that instrumentation is never a matter of selecting colors as such, but a matter of 'setting,' of composing in a way that really activates each instrument. The task is not to compose ordinary music for unusual instruments; it is more important to compose unusual music for ordinary instruments. This refers not only to the structure of the music, but above all to the particular gift of 'inventing' in a specific instrumental sense. As a rule, chamber-music ensembles require compositions in a truly chamber-music style. The ordinary salon-orchestra composing is unsuitable for such an ensemble. The piano or novachord part must be treated soloistically; its purpose should not be merely to indicate the harmony.

Composing and Recording

The principal factor to be considered here is synchronization. The music must hit definite points, the time of the music and the picture must coincide down to the last detail. Consequently, the music must be flexible, so that occasionally whole bars or phrases can be omitted, added, or repeated; the composer must keep in mind the possibility of fermatas and rubati; he must have at his command a certain amount of planned improvisation – the opposite of bad, accidental improvised composing – in order to achieve complete synchronization and a lively performance. Examples of such planned improvisation can be found particularly in operatic music.

Despite this the conductor is sometimes compelled to slow up or accelerate the music for the sake of improving synchronization. If this occurs, the music becomes distorted and senseless. Although experienced composers and conductors try to avoid such accidental distortions, ritenuti and accelerandi are only too often used without any real justification. The same fault can be observed in poor performances of advanced modern music.

In long sequences requiring the continuous coincidence of pictures and music, synchronization must be automatized. To obtain mathematical exactness, the inability of human beings to observe mechanical time relations must be corrected by mechanical devices. Rhythmograms enable the composer at his desk to see, for instance, that clouds drift across the screen from the second quarter note of the first bar to the third quarter note of the fourteenth, and that between the first and the third quarters of the twelfth bar the heroine raises her hand. Thus he can write a score that follows every detail, however complicated and differentiated, with the utmost precision. In such a score all modifications of tempo must be clearly worked out; they are no longer subject to the whims of a conductor or the constraint of synchronization. The conductor merely controls and rehearses, he no longer interprets the music.

This type of technique affects the character of the music, excluding all 'fluid,' contingent elements. Utmost accuracy of structure from the smallest detail to the complete work is a paramount consideration. The music must run like clockwork, the art of composing here consists in meaningfully relating all the minute and often divergent details. It goes without saying that such music is cool and remote rather than expressive.

The general technical level of musical recording is astonishingly high, considering that the sound film has existed only a short time. However, the apparatus is still deficient in many important respects. First of all, the basic noise accompanying every sound film is still too loud. Further, the total sound has no spatial depth, and the music is flat, with a foreground character, as though it were perceived with only one ear. For this reason, densely scored pieces are difficult to record clearly. The 16-foot sound tones (double-bass, tuba, contrabassoon) and the highest registers (piccolo) are still less sure than the middle register. While many of these defects could be eliminated by greater care, more generous expenditure of time, and other reforms of the studio routine, a decisive advance can be made only on the basis of new technical standards, not through isolated efforts. Science has already made these standards possible, but the industry has not taken them over for fear of having to make new investments – every movie theater would have to install a new projecting machine. The procedure applied by Disney in the otherwise questionable film *Fantasia*, which he called 'fantasy-sound,' gives an idea of the new technique.

Composers of cinema music are exposed to a special danger that other composers hardly ever have to face: arbitrary cuts made by the film director when he dislikes something, when any sound contradicts his conventional ideal of beauty, or simply when a passage involves difficult problems for the instrumentalists, so that rehearsing would take too much time. Such cuts are made with total disregard of musical logic, and the composer's position in the industry is such that his protestations have no chance of being heard, let alone heeded. This practice is another reason for what we have called planned improvisation, i.e., for writing a type of music that would not be thrown completely out of gear by certain anticipated cuts. The situation of music as a secondary, auxiliary means is painfully manifested here by such threats and by its frequent distortion through inadequate performance. Under the prevailing conditions, the only thing the composer can do about it is to be as careful as possible with regard to the safety of his 'setting,' that is, he not only must avoid writing any bar unless he can accurately imagine its sound, but must also be sure that everything he writes is fully realizable under the average conditions of performance. It goes without saying that such self-restraint constantly impedes the freedom of his imagination.

Conductors and Musicians

As a rule the cinema studios do not follow the practice of European opera houses, which hire talented young musicians after they have finished their schooling. Conducting jobs still go to conventional performers from night clubs or musical shows, or to orchestra players who have worked their way up through diligence or connections, unless it is the composer himself who directs his own works for better or for worse. The ordinary conductors of motion-picture orchestras replace genuine musical experience and knowledge with the habit of automatic adjustment to the conditions of recording and particularly synchronization. As a rule they do not know how to rehearse or, often, even how to beat time properly; they merely keep the orchestra going with a minimum of preparation. With all this they maintain the fiction that they are experts whose knowledge is something quite different from ordinary musicianship.

It must be granted that the working conditions of the studio conductor hardly permit of adequate performances. Awareness that each additional hour of rehearsal or recording means additional expense puts the conductor under permanent pressure, and, as is the case in all hierarchies, he merely transmits this pressure when he proceeds autocratically. The whole process of production is marked by haste; the composer must work from hand to mouth, the conductor has hardly any time to study his score, and if he is compelled to do so he usually cannot go beyond the most primitive task of synchronization, the providing of cues at the proper times. Since he must make use of every minute, both he and the orchestra are tremendously overburdened. Quite often he must assimilate the freshly copied music only during rehearsal and have it played long enough to cement it together somehow, and this again means loss of time for real rehearsing.

The level of the orchestra players is, on the contrary, very high. The best instrumentalists try to obtain work in the studios for pecuniary reasons. But they have to pay a high price for the money they earn. They suffer from the unworthy and often unendurably shabby cinema scores they must play, from a regime that combines senseless pedantry with irresponsible bungling, and from the inadequacy of the conductors. Particular hardships are imposed by the absurd and inconsiderate working hours, which result more from incompetence than from necessity. The musicians are summoned at the most inconvenient hours, often in the middle of the night; they are made to play until they are completely exhausted, in extreme cases the same miserable sixteen measures for eight hours on end, while problems concerning the performance of difficult music are often ignored for lack of time. Short periods of inhuman strain are often followed by weeks of idleness. (Incidentally, such practices are among the most demoralizing in the whole cinema industry.) The gifts of the musicians are wasted and ruined. They become insensitive and indifferent, and are actually trained to be careless. In self-defense they end up by assuming an attitude of silent contempt toward the whole business. They vent their resentment on everything difficult and unusual, that is to say particularly on modern music, which should expect to find its best allies among the objectively oriented orchestra musicians. Instead, they react coolly to unusual sounds and applaud when a brilliant E-major seems felicitous.

7
Suggestions and Conclusions

Suggestions for improving the quality and the methods of using motion-picture music are naturally open to suspicion. The cultural industry as a whole, and particularly the realm of motion-picture music, is characterized by the fact that all the people concerned in it are fully aware of its defects and often denounce them; at the same time, any innovation, even the most modest, that is not in complete conformity with the prevailing trend encounters the most stubborn opposition, which defies the best intentions. What is in question here is not the arbitrary decisions of the 'big bosses' – these are invoked only in extreme cases, because anyone who enters the lion's den is so resigned and prepared to adjust himself to reality that dramatic clashes are ruled out in advance. The artists know that any reference to art is apt to infuriate the management, and that showmanship and box-office receipts must be accepted explicitly or implicitly as the guideposts of their work.

However, even within the limits set by showmanship and box-office success, every genuine innovation meets with opposition that manifests itself not as censorship, but as inertia, as the rule of 'common sense' in a thousand little matters, or as respect for allegedly irrefutable experience.

Attempts at reform degenerate into guerilla warfare, and in the end break down completely because of the disproportion between the hypertrophied power of a system rationalized to the point of absurdity, and any possible individual initiative – not because of objections on the part of the executive, who intervenes only occasionally, to teach the artist that he is only a cipher.

There are various ways of adjusting oneself to this situation. Some –

those who are most successful from the pecuniary point of view – go over to the enemy and embrace the cause that they hate; they see in the mass base of the motion picture a guarantee of its truth; they declare solemnly that the artist can do anything, no matter how audacious, provided that he knows his trade, and use their spurious authority as experts to throttle the boldness in others that they themselves dare not display. Others are vociferous in their disapproval; rebel, claim to be enemies of the whole business; but in the end their products are curiously like those of the people they profess to despise. Still others – the intellectuals of the motion-picture world – adopt an extremist attitude and decide that the motion-picture industry has nothing to do with art, and that culture is doomed in any event. This idea is used as an all-embracing mental reservation, which enables them to yield in every detail while preserving their good conscience. Such people are even more cynical than the businessmen. Proud of their superior knowledge, they discourage every would-be innovator by giving him a hundred reasons why his proposals must fail. In their priggishness and learned conceit they condemn the naive reformer on the ground that he is resorting to patchwork instead of doing a thorough job.

While it is indisputable that even the most insignificant defects are inseparable from the inadequacy of the whole system, theoretical criticism of fundamentals should not be misused as a letter of indulgence with regard to practice. Irresponsible radicalism of summary rejection is not an infantile disease but a symptom of senile weakness in those who are weary of futile opposition. To have a clear insight into the true nature of the causes of the present evil and to refuse to indulge in the illusion that the system can be changed by gradual corrections does not necessarily mean that one must give up all efforts to bring about a better state of affairs. Such efforts will not suffice to emancipate the musical motion picture but they can give an idea of what the emancipated motion picture would look like.

Even at the price of daily quarrels with wretched opponents, it is of great importance that an unofficial tradition of genuine art be formed which may one day make itself felt. For the new motion picture cannot fall from heaven; its history which has not yet really begun will be largely determined by its prehistory. The specific requirements of the material that seem to have a hindering effect in many respects in other respects bring pressure to bear in the direction of emancipation against the intentions of the producers and consumers. When subject matter, however unworthy it may be, is approached objectively, an element of truth is introduced that asserts itself against the existing limitations. This element is contained in the present practices in a fragmentary and anonymous form; it must be brought to consciousness and consciously furthered.

As regards motion-picture music, the possibilities of improvement are considerably narrowed down, aside from the general conditions of production, by a far more primitive factor, namely, the present nature of motion-picture material pictures and dialogues. Fundamentally, no motion-picture music can be better than what it accompanies. Music for a trashy picture is to some extent trashy, no matter how elegantly or skilfully it has solved its problems. The postulate that the music must always have some sort of relation to the picture on the screen defines its limits; it must follow the lead of the inferior material to which it is subordinated. Good music accompanying hackneyed or idiotic action and meaningless chatter becomes bad and meaningless – and this does not mean that a music as bad as the picture is more adequate.

It is true that occasionally skilfully composed music can rebel and disavow the picture that degrades it, either by ruthless opposition or by revealing exaggeration. But the value of such stratagems must not be overestimated, any more than that of artistic sabotage in general. Under the present cultural conditions, they would hardly be noticed by the public, and would usually be nipped in the bud by the agencies of control within the industry. And even if such extraordinary *tours de force* could get across, they would remain exceptions that prove the rule. They would degenerate into specialized and ingenious applied art, adding a 'sophisticated touch.' Harsh music accompanying a post-card love scene, for instance, would not merely contrast with it and result in a presumably comical effect of the whole; it would also be ridiculous, naive, and futile. Intended to convict the motion picture of banality, it would itself be convicted of uselessly wasting energy. Likewise, bold musical colors, whether of harmony or instrumentation, would be disfigured when associated with sugary sweet technicolor. Far from 'refuting' technicolor, they themselves would sound 'dirty,' by virtue of the contrast, no matter how purely they were set forth or how shoddy the visual glamor on the screen. Most important, however, is the fact that the seriousness of the musical tone becomes spurious when associated with the show. In claiming to be something that is compatible with the picture, it loses all right to function as purely musical expression. In a conventional film, conventional, essentially spurious music can occasionally be 'truer' than genuine music, because the former at least does not degrade truth into an element of spuriousness.

One does not necessarily sanction the complacency of zealous writers of music when one holds that improvement of motion-picture music is inseparable from improvement of the motion picture, that it cannot be undertaken as an isolated specialized venture. However, the following considerations do not take the motion picture itself into account, and are deliberately confined to problems of motion-picture music that reflect the disease of the macrocosm of which it is part.

Technique and Spirit

Superficially considered, the defects of cinema music fall into two groups. First, there are the technical imperfections of all kinds: barbaric vestiges of the early period of motion pictures; avoidable irrationalities of management and working methods; backward machinery and procedures that are still used out of parsimony, despite the prevailing infatuation with inventions and gadgets – in brief, everything that is incompatible with the spirit of technological progress. Second, there are the defects stemming from social and economic sources: deference to the market, particularly to infantile and immature consumers whose bad taste is often enough a mere pretext for the producers; the unconscious will to conform and agree with established norms in every realm, even where the remotest problems of musical structure are concerned; the deep-rooted tendency to frustration – the consumer, instead of receiving something genuinely and substantially new, for which he may be unconsciously yearning, is fed on the endless repetition of the habitual. It is generally believed that the first group of defects might be corrected automatically with the growing rationalization of the industry – this would be progress consisting in the elimination of out-of-date and accidental elements; as for those of the second group, they are believed to be irremediable, and bound to grow in strength. The implicit critique of the motion picture as contained in Huxley's negative utopia, *Brave New World*, seems to reflect this judgment. In this novel, the talkies are superseded by the 'feelies' which enable the spectator to experience all the physical sensations shown on the screen – he not only can sample the kisses of his favorite stars, but, greatest triumph of all, he can touch every single hair in the picture of a bearskin; but the content of the 'feelies' is completely moronic, even worse than that of today's pictures, if possible.

However plausible this prognosis may sound, however blatant the contradiction between the technique of reproduction and the content of the pictures, such interpretations oversimplify the facts of the case and lead to romantic distortions. Technical and intellectual inadequacies cannot be mechanically divided. Thus the phenomenon of neutralization discussed in chapter 5, which contributes so much to endowing motion-picture music with the character of a 'digest' of material pre-digested by the machinery, and to bringing it down to the intellectual level of all the other elements involved, cannot be separated from the technique of the recording procedures; if the latter is thoroughly transformed, the meaning of the music and even its social bearing may very well be affected. On the other hand, the seemingly technical backwardness of motion-picture music as manifested in many ways, from the taboo against modern musical resources to the vested privileges of incompetent routinists, is determined by speculation on public taste, by the night-club hedonism of those in control, and by the peculiar social structure of the industry; and there is no symptom that the internal growth of the musico-technological forces automatically does away with all this.

Within the motion-picture concerns that have developed in planless competition, spirit and technique appear as alien to one another, and their relationship as one of blind arbitrariness. But socially, these two elements are connected by multiple channels, and although they contradict one another, they are inextricably mingled and interdetermined. The development of technology affects the spirit as much as the spirit affects the selection, direction, and impeding of technological processes. There is no absolute gull between technical innovations and intellectual reforms, superficial changes and profound transformations, practical and utopian proposals. In a petrified and stationary system the most practical idea may seem eccentric, and at the same time the most extravagant fantasy can come close to realization, thanks to a sudden technical advance.

Artistic Objectivity and Public

We must repeat that the use of music in motion pictures should be inspired by objective considerations, by the intrinsic requirements of the work. However, after having shown in detail how preoccupation with the audience spoils cinema music, we wish to state here that the relation between the objective requirements and the effect on the audience is not one of simple opposition, and that there is an ingredient of truth in what the public expects of the cinema. Even under the regime of the industry, the public has not become a mere machine recording facts and figures; behind the shell of conventionalized behavior patterns, resistance and spontaneity still survive. To imagine that the demands of the public are always 'bad' and the views of the experts always 'good' is to indulge in dangerous oversimplification. It must not be forgotten that the notion of 'the expert' is part of the same machinery that has reduced art to an administrative and commercial matter. The argument of the advocates of the existing motion-picture music is: 'The people want to have it this way, otherwise the thing won't go' – in other words, they invoke the expert's appraisal of the audience, which always amounts to shrewd manipulation of the public. To subject cinema music to objective requirements is to represent the public's objective interests as against its manipulated interests, with regard to which the public is merely the customer.

Thus, the public's vague awareness that music should come to the aid of the picture, that it should 'motivate' the events on the screen, is legitimate. The industry takes this desire into account, but misuses the music in order to give a technically mediated factor the appearance of immediacy. This ideological function is so close to the true and genuine one that it is practically impossible to set up an abstract criterion for distinguishing between the objectively warranted use of music and its bad use for purposes of glorification. Likewise, the public's general attitude expresses both the human desire for music and the troubled need to escape, and no individual audience reaction can be subsumed under one or the other category. The only possible method is to determine in each individual case, on the basis of the function and nature of the music, to what extent it actually fulfils its mission or to what extent its humanity is used only to mask the inhuman.

A more specific principle is that the music should not over-eagerly identify itself with the event on the screen or its mood, but should be able to assert its distance from them and thus accentuate the general meaning. But even such a use of music is not a panacea; the fraud might very well come in at that point. It will have to be decided in each case with what the music has identified itself and whether the identification – for instance, with the despair of the characters on the screen – is actually achieved or replaced with clichés, which temper this despair and bring it down to the level of conventionally allowed emotions. However, the public is always right in experiencing as boredom what was described, from an objective standpoint, as 'unrelated' music. Even here it should be noted that today almost every product of the cultural industry is objectively boring, but that the psycho-technique of the studios deprives the consumers of the awareness of the boredom they experience.

In the prevailing practice, the effect on the spectator is planned while the content of the music is planless. The situation should be reversed. The music should be planned without an eye for the effect, and then the public will get its due. Genuine planning is concerned with the relation between picture and music and the structure of the music itself. Today the music imitates the play on the screen, the picture, and yet the greater the effort to assimilate the two media the more hopelessly they are split apart. The important task is to establish fruitful tensions between them. A proper dramaturgy, the unfolding of a general meaning, would sharply distinguish among pictures, words, and music, and for that very reason relate them meaningfully to one another.

As compared to the prevailing conditions, the music should in some respects be brought closer to the motion picture and in other respects taken further from it. It should not be a mere additional stimulus, as it is in a farce with songs and dances, a kind of next course in a dinner, or another 'feature'; on the contrary, it should at every moment be an integral part of the picture as a whole. However, it should not be its automatic duplication, it should not decrease the distance between picture and spectator by creating moods; but by virtue of its character of immediacy – and music still possesses this character to a greater extent than any other art – it should stress the mediated and alienated elements in the photographed action and the recorded words, thus preventing confusion between reality and reproduction, a confusion that is all the more dangerous because the reproduction appears to be more similar to reality than it ever was.

'It's Non-commercial'

The film industry opposes objective innovations in the music chiefly on the ground that they would compromise box-office receipts and go against the public's wishes, which the industry has allegedly ascertained, although not even ordinary market research has been carried through in this field. The standard argument against modern music, 'it is non-commercial,' can be challenged on the ground that so-called non-commercial music has never been given a serious trial; that prejudice has made it impossible to discover whether it is really as non-commercial as all that, or whether on the contrary, by breaking through the universal boredom, it would not increase box-office receipts to the discomfiture of the old-timers. Take, for instance, Edmund Meisel's music to *Potemkin*. Meisel was only a modest composer, and his score is certainly not a masterpiece; however, it was non-commercial at the time it was written, it avoided the neutralizing clichés and preserved a certain striking power, however crude. Nevertheless there is not the slightest indication that its aggressiveness impaired its effectiveness to the public; on the contrary, its effectiveness was enhanced.

Other instances, too, prove that when, by way of exception, serious composers have been permitted to write for cinemas, there was no outbreak of panic among the audience. But until a large-scale experiment with advanced music, masterfully composed and constructed, is made within the big companies and their distributive apparatus – and is made without the mental reservation that it is destined only for highbrows – the thesis that decent and advanced music is non-commercial is nothing but an empty phrase, which serves only to cover up the laziness, slovenliness, and ignorance of vested privilege, and the abominable cult of the average.

New music could indeed be conspicuous, but only in a fundamentally transformed, de-standardized motion picture. The usual argument that new music is unsaleable refutes itself when applied to the prevailing practice, for in today's motion pictures the music is so little noticed that its nature is almost a matter of indifference. The average moviegoer is hardly ever aware of the music, and probably he would be even less aware of the degree of its modernism. This is, of course, no argument for the use of modern music, because it might easily be replied that since the type of music used is a matter of indifference, one might as well continue the existing state of affairs, and even add that radical music would only be dishonored if it were tolerated by the industry. However, such considerations involve the admission that the notion of 'poison for the box office' should not be taken as seriously as all that. And those who advocate attempts to carry out as many innovations as possible within the existing framework, to serve as an eventual starting point for a fundamentally changed motion picture, certainly have the right to insist that the experiments should also include resources and techniques that for the time being cannot fulfil their proper function, and even those that are still in a rudimentary phase of development.

Specificity and Routine

Whatever the nature of the resources used, motion-picture music should be specific, derived from the particular conditions of the given case, and should not be taken out of the storeroom, in the literal and figurative meaning of this term. When a director makes a picture of anti-Nazi resistance in a country invaded by Hitler, he takes great pains to see to it that the telephone receivers are exactly of the kind used in that country, and that the uniforms of the Elite Guards conform in every detail to the actual garb. Since this kind of surface accuracy is generally achieved at the cost of all genuine political and social plausibility, it is ridiculous and disgusting. But cinema music has not even reached the level of that accuracy. The question is not raised whether it coincides to some extent with even the most trivial interpretation of the subject, let alone whether it expresses any truth of a higher order. To grab what is nearest at hand is considered the best procedure when music is concerned – it is as though, in our example, the director dressed his Elite Guard leaders in the uniforms of the American Coast Guard, simply because they happened to be available.

In other words, motion-picture music falls short even of the miserable standards of the art of make-up, without having anything good by the fact that it lags behind the bad. Guerilla heroes in Hollywood garb may be spurious, but to accompany them with the music of a European masked ball of 1880 is more spurious. Before the emancipation of motion-picture music can be discussed at all, it must rid itself of the musical horse-and-buggy atmosphere. This does not mean that music would have to catch up with all the stupidities of literal imitation in order to acquire strength – for instance, that the Elite Guard in our example would have to bleat out the latest Nazi hit. But cinema music will not even begin to improve until every single sequence is treated with exact regard to its special function. Within the existing framework, the most important requirement is to cut through the associative automatism, which always employs a hackneyed type of music for a given sequence, according to the pattern: 'let's have more of the same.' Even the worst music that escapes from this constraint would be better than the routine material that complies with it.

Another requirement, closely related to the preceding, is that no 'rules of experience' should be recognized until they have been tried out. When there is no genuine experience there can be no rules. Not even the habitual practices have been developed in a consistent and progressive manner. The approved rules are nothing but the definitions that circumscribe the musical horizon of the department heads. The struggle against them constitutes the composer's martyrdom in his actual work. Now, one should not cherish any illusions about the alleged power of the personality in asserting itself against the industry. Nevertheless, one should not consider the composer's struggle against common nonsense completely hopeless. For there is at least one realm in which the will of the low-grade businessman and that of the artist are commensurable over short stretches: the realm of technique. Those who have seen how orchestra players, who perform only reluctantly an advanced modern work under a conductor unsympathetic to and intellectually suspicious of modern music, change their attitude the moment they realize that another conductor knows the score and handles it with the same precision as a traditional one and that it has meaning in his hands know where the opportunity lies for an uncompromising composer in motion pictures. Masterful handling of resources carries a certain weight of its own even when it is directed against every idea tolerated by the industry. Orchestra players are in spite of everything most sensitive to it and their confidence spreads under certain circumstances to everyone concerned with the production of the picture.

The responsible composer can assert himself against convention once he gives striking proof that he knows more than the routinist. It is difficult to define in advance what this kind of knowledge is – it refers to a certain familiarity with the sensuous practical aspect of music, to the ability to 'realize.' To be sure, technical competence that arouses confidence can degenerate into professional automatism and lead to ultimate subordination to a routine; yet in it lies the only possibility of asserting the new. This possibility is enhanced by the circumstance that actually the critical and advanced musician is to a large extent also objectively more competent even though he is often less 'practical.' It follows that the composer has the duty to translate all his aesthetic and dramatic insights, however speculative they may be, into technical problems. A good deal of the technology of the industrialized work of art is inflated and pretentious; but the composer proves his superiority only by measuring himself against technology, not by abstractly and nobly negating it. If he opposes to the director or producer general considerations about good and bad modern and reactionary music, he remains helpless, and his cause is ridiculed with him. But if, against the conventional ideas of his employers, he writes a composition more effective than the one they have imagined, which fulfils its function more exactly than the one they wanted him to compose, he may prevail.

Discretion

A fundamental requirement that taxes all of a composer's sensitiveness is that he should not write a single sequence, not even a single note, that overlooks the social-technological prerequisite of the motion picture, namely, its nature as mass production. No motion-picture music should have the same character of uniqueness that is desirable in music intended for live performance. In other words, motion-picture music should not become the tool of pseudo-individualization.[1] But therein the greatest, almost insurmountable difficulties are involved. First of all, music, by its nature and origin, seems inseparable from the factor of uniqueness, the *hic et nunc*. The occurrence of the same music in different places at the same time, especially when the intimacy of the moment, its whim, so to speak, is emphasized, implies something that is almost anti-musical, as manifested most clearly in motion pictures of concerts.[2] As a matter of fact, the motion picture itself consists of mass reproductions of unique events, and thus compels the composer to deal with individual situations, whose very nature resists such mass reproduction.

There is no sense in covering up such contradictions, the profoundest that confront motion-picture music, far beyond the bounds of the existing practices; on the contrary they should be made apparent. And since the composer cannot evade them, they should enter as an element into his music. The aim is to write music that abandons itself to its concrete occasion as 'unique' – and this is the basic postulate of specific composing – but at the same time takes care not to seek its fulfilment in the triumph of intruding upon something 'unique.' One might almost say that the profoundest requirement of cinema music is that of 'discretion' – namely, that it should not behave indiscreetly with regard to its object, that it should not suggest close intimacy, but that on the contrary it should mitigate the inevitable impression of embarrassing closeness to an intimate event, which every motion picture produces. This is the contemporary form of musical 'taste,' and the picture itself can teach us something in this respect. Thus, the portrayal of the departure of a ship and the crowded pier is rightly considered more appropriate than close-ups of kisses; the reason for this is not prudishness, but the circumstance that in the ship scene the element of the uniqueness, of the *hic et nunc*, although present, is not as pronounced and does not affect the picture to the same extent as in the picture of a lover's embrace. The cinema composer who in a sense is constantly driven to behave in the manner of people kissing in public should heed this lesson. From the point of view of advanced composing, music illustrating a noisy crowd seems more appropriate than music illustrating an erotic scene. It is said that a contract with Stravinsky was canceled because he stipulated that he would not illustrate any love scenes.

The paradox inherent in motion-picture music – the fact that it is both technified and obliged to have a character of uniqueness – if it is really as inevitable as it appears to be – leads to a fundamental consequence concerning the general attitude of the music. Being a 'multipliable unique' it is always supposed to achieve what it actually cannot achieve. It must give a hint to this situation unless it is blindly to succumb to this contradiction. In other words, motion-picture music must not take itself seriously in the same way as autonomous music does. Analysis of the most fundamental premises of motion-picture music thus confirms what we have inferred from the fact of its subordination to its purpose and the impossibility of its autonomous development. With some exaggeration it may be said that essentially all motion-picture music contains an element of humor, speaks with its tongue in its cheek, as it were, and that it degenerates into a bad kind of naïveté as soon as it forgets this element.

It is hardly an accident that the music for those pictures in which the idea of technification has made the greatest inroads on the function of music, that is, the cartoons, almost always takes on the aspect of a joke through the use of sound effects. The investigations made by the Film Music Project show that almost all new and unconventional solutions are based on ideas that are at least close to humorous elements. This should not be misunderstood. What is advocated here is not that the music as such should have a facetious character; on the contrary, it should make use of the whole gamut of expression. Nor should the music necessarily make mock of the events on the screen. The element of humor is rather to be found in the formal relation of the music to its object and in its function.

For instance (we refer here to an example studied by the Project), the music imitates caution. Actually, this is impossible; caution is a specific human behavior, and music cannot express it and accurately distinguish it from similar impulses without the help of concepts. The music is aware of this, and exaggerates itself in order to enforce the association of caution, which it actually cannot express. Thereby it ceases to take itself literally in its immediacy; it turns into a joke something that it cannot do seriously. By doing this, it suspends the claim of the physical immediacy of the *hic et nunc*, which is incompatible with its technological situation. By keeping itself at a distance, it also creates a distance from its place and hour.

Something of this element – the formal self-negation of music that plays with itself – should be present in every composition for motion pictures as an antidote against the danger of pseudo-individualization. The postulate of universal planning leads of itself to such functional jokes, which at the same time are inseparable from technification. The very fact that something is mechanically manufactured and is at the same time music objectively implies a comical element. Music will escape being comical involuntarily only by agreeing to be comical voluntarily. The formal facetious function is nothing but the awareness of music that it is mediated, technically produced, and reproduced. In a certain sense, every productive dramatic musical idea in the motion picture is a paradox. It hardly needs to be shown that such an affinity to jokes reflects the deepest unconscious tensions in the audience's reaction to motion-picture music.[3]

The same problem can be approached from a different angle – in relation to the effect of music, which is today the exclusive consideration, and which, despite its questionableness, is nevertheless always to some extent revealing objectively. Cinema music is not carefully listened to. If this fact is more or less accepted as an inevitable premise, the best of which has to be made, the aim will be to compose music that, even though it is listened to inattentively, can as a whole be perceived correctly and adequately to its function, without having to move along beaten associative tracks that help the listener to grasp the music, but block any adequate fulfilment of its function. The composer is thus faced with a new and strange task – that of producing something sensible, which at the same time can be perceived by way of parenthesis, as it slips by the listener. Such a requirement is closely related to that of music that does not take itself seriously. Good cinema music must achieve everything that it does achieve on the surface, so to speak; it must not become lost in itself. Its whole structure – and it needs structure more than any form of autonomous music – must become visible; and the more it adds the lacking depth dimension to the picture, the less it must itself develop in depth. This is not meant in the sense of musical 'superficiality'; on the contrary it is precisely the procedure diametrically opposed to the superficial, fleeting, and comfortable convention. It implies the striving to make everything completely sensuous, in contrast to musical transcendence and inwardness. In technical terms, this means the predominance of movement and color over the musical depth dimension, harmony, which governs just the conventional patterns.

Cinema music should sparkle and glisten. It should attain the quick pace of the casual listening imposed by the picture, and not be left behind. Tonal colors can be perceived faster and with less effort than harmonies, unless the latter follow the tonal pattern and. are therefore not registered at all as specific. Sparkling variation and coloristic richness are also most readily compatible with technification. By displaying a tendency to vanish as soon as it appears, motion-picture music renounces its claim that it is *there*, which is today its cardinal sin.

Appendix
Report on the Film Music Project

The purpose of this appendix is not to report on a project that can be judged only on the basis of its concrete results as regards cinema music, and even less to present these results as a model for the correct procedure,. but to illustrate the thesis of the present book, especially the formulations of the last chapter, down to details of composition.

The limitations of what has been achieved are clear enough. If modesty must be required of cinema music, then this quality is even more necessary in regard to attempts that diverge in their most significant aspect from commercial pictures, namely, by the absence of business control. Outside the studios, innovations such as those to be discussed here are not only suspected of being the fruits of utopianism nurtured in an artificial preserve, but in addition the outside situation manifests itself objectively as the isolation of the experiments from the production process of the motion picture and in a certain arbitrariness of the whole approach, which is as remote from real planning as the practice of the studios.

In other words, we are dealing not with 'positive solutions,' but rather with potentialities that are opened up under both exceptionally favorable and limiting conditions and that might become fertile outside the zone protected against the market. The idea of a 'positive solution' should be treated with reserve under the prevailing assumptions anyway: usually it amounts merely to smug conformity, rationalized by the dubious excuse that it is always better to do something than nothing at all. What is important, however, is not contributions and attempts at patching up things, but formulations of problems which start from the existing praxis, and which lead of themselves to its reversal. In brief, the aim has been to find out how a conscious formulation of the tasks of motion-picture music becomes manifest in the material, and this refers both to the pictorial element which is taken as is, and to the compositional which is treated critically. The purpose of the project was completely experimental.

Here prejudices and bad habits had not to be taken for granted. Even where they seem to be a matter of plain common sense, they had to be ruled out. Their hackneyed stereotype would reduce their effect to naught even when they made sense in themselves. The only criterion was dramaturgy, that is, the function of the music in the film as a whole. At all times the composer tried to go to the very bottom of the problem of the dramaturgic relation between music and motion pictures, to test extreme instances of this relation: resemblance and contrast, warming up and cooling down, distance and proximity, and in doing this to gain an insight into the most adequate procedure for each case. In this task the new musical material was helpful. But it, too, was subordinated to the primacy of the dramaturgic and was not used indiscriminately in the manner of a composer writing autonomous music, but viewed in accordance with functional requirements. The question in regard to simplicity or complexity upon which the character of each piece depends was, like any other, determined by the over-all plan.

Sociological considerations were taken into account at least in so far as strips serving in any way the ideology propagated by cultural industry were eliminated. It goes without saying that the music everywhere avoided to advertise the 'moods' of the picture – a function that is generally attributed to it by business routine.

The aesthetic intention was to keep the style of the music flexible without, however, falling into eclecticism. The composer was guided by his confidence in his 'touch': a manner that is sufficiently developed to impose itself in seemingly divergent stylistic fields and give them the stamp of unity. Achieving a specific relation between each sequence and its music was put above every other aim.

As regards the composition technique – in the sense of 'planning' – attention was above all given to form problems, to 'architecture.' This was a result both of the necessary restraint in other musical dimensions, especially the contrapuntal one, and the dramaturgic function, which in each case starts from certain structural units of action and contexts that are reflected by the build-up of the music. However, other tasks, such as strictly synchronistic composing aiming at 'points,' and thereby the principle of motion-picture music 'pointing,' were by no means neglected.

Thus the experiments of the project were not specialized or reduced to the compositional aspect, but touched upon all problems of motion-picture music. Therein, in emancipation of music from compartmentalized thinking, lay its novelty; and the musical results achieved are due as much to this conception of the film as a unity composed of heterogeneous elements, as to the composer's interest in the tendencies of modern music.

Sociological investigations might have been undertaken in connection with the general plan of the project. For instance, some of the feature-film sequences could have been performed for different groups of listeners, accompanied sometimes by the old music and sometimes by that worked out in the project, and the reactions could have been studied under laboratory conditions, by means of questionnaires and interviews. But such investigations lay outside the scope of the project; moreover, their results would merely contribute data concerning the possible mass audience reactions to the use of modern music in motion pictures. Nevertheless, it would be worthwhile to ascertain whether the motion-picture audience's aversion to modern music is not merely a legend, and whether it would not approve of modern music that adequately fulfilled its dramatic function. Such proof might help to break down the prejudice against modem music in the film industry.

The Project

In the spring of 1940, the Rockefeller Foundation granted the New School for Social Research the sum of $20,000 for systematic research in motion-picture music. The New School appointed Hanns Eisler as director of this project, which originally was to last two years. Later, the period was extended by nine months.

The basic idea of this undertaking was to apply the new musical resources, as discussed in chapter 3, to motion pictures. More particularly, methods were to be studied for closing the gap between the highly evolved technique of the motion picture and the generally far less advanced technique of motion-picture music. Attention was focused at first on practical experiments, rather than on theory. Only after the completion of the project were the results analyzed and incorporated into the present book.

Although the project was entirely independent of the motion-picture industry, the latter showed its interest in the project by releasing film material for the experiments. Such material was submitted by Walter Wanger, Twentieth Century-Fox, Paramount, March of Time, Frontier Films, and by Josef Losey and Joris Ivens, independent producers.

Because the project had to content itself with the available material, certain difficulties arose. Scenes severed from their context often lost the meaning they had had as parts of a whole, and dramatic planning, as discussed in the chapter on aesthetics, was narrowly restricted. Documentary material predominated; but this was not a disadvantage. In the prevailing type of feature films, music that represents more than a background frequently appears in sequences with a documentary character, such as scenes from 'nature,' panoramas of cities, and moments in the plot when the action is suspended and the spectator's attention is directed to something more universal. Although much of this practice is a bad convention, it is reasonable, in so far as action, whenever it is concentrated in the dialogue – and this is still true of most feature pictures – is difficult to combine with music. The wretchedly blurred character of the usual background music suffices to illustrate this.

Conversely, newsreel sequences often seem to be broken-off fragments of feature films. Thus, even though the project, because of the looseness of its connections with Hollywood business, was largely confined to documentary sequences, it could study problems relating to feature films. The fragmentary feature-film material was astonishingly similar to the documentary material.

Methods

The practical work was divided into the following stages:

(1) Composing. Experiments were conducted exclusively with new compositions written expressly for the project and used with the available picture sequences. Hanns Eisler composed all the scores.

(2) Recording. This was done under the direction of conductors who were particularly well-qualified to interpret advanced music.

(3) Cutting, mixing, and editing. The same working processes were applied to experimental material as are applied to regular motion pictures. Timing also followed the usual practices, since the purpose was to make sure that the new results could be used in the production of

films under present-day conditions. Even the time spent on composing conformed to the average situation prevailing in the motion-picture industry.

The following sequences were used:

(1) Scenes in a children's camp (performance time 22 minutes): Camp life is shown in its various aspects: sports, handicrafts, tending animals, quarrels, eating, sleeping.

(2) Nature scenes (18 minutes): Eruption of a volcano, a blizzard, the collapse of an iceberg in the Arctic. The material produced a wide range of expression.

(3) Fourteen ways of describing rain (14 minutes): New music composed for Joris Ivens' *Rain*, with a great variety of rain effects.

(4) Excerpts from weekly newsreels (14 minutes): War scenes.

(5) Sequences from feature films (14 minutes): Excerpts from *Grapes of Wrath* and *Forgotten Village*.

The total performance time of the compositions was 82 minutes.

Survey of the Work Done

The Children's Camp has no plot; it is a loose sequence of somewhat genre-like pictures that are held together by the common scene of action, a camp. The whole is simple and unpretentious. Josef Losey, the director, clearly distinguished the scenes; each deals with a special phase of camp life, and each is designed to make a special point. The relative lengths of the scenes were carefully balanced.

The musical problem was to save the picture from the usual saccharine sentimental and humorous romanticism of magazine stories about children. The effect of the music could be neither stirring nor funny. Its range of feeling had to include elements that usually are not associated with children: genuine seriousness, such as children often show in their play; sadness, nervousness, even hysteria; but all this conceived loosely, thinly, as though inconsequentially. Above all, the music should not tap the children on the shoulder, as it were, and make them the object of adults' jokes or ingratiate itself by adopting a spurious baby talk.

The form of the suite seemed most natural – in other words, not an elaborate form with transitions and maybe leitmotifs, but a sequence of small, distinct, clearly differentiated pieces, each complete in itself with an unmistakable beginning and ending.

American nursery rhymes – 'Strawberry Fair,' 'Sourwood Mountain,' 'Little Ah Sid,' and others – supplied a musical raw material that was suitable because of its simplicity and associations. Eisler also wished to show that it is possible to write unconventional music even with the simplest material constructively differentiated, without the need of pretentious disguise.

The score calls for seven solo instruments – flute, clarinet, bassoon, and string quartet. The style is that of chamber music, with the instruments alternately prominent, but without any developed polyphony. Harmonically it never goes beyond the limits of tonality, although it uses all the steps of the chromatic scale as independent progressions.

Some characteristic passages are noteworthy. A short allegretto introduction accompanying the film title gives the keynote. It contains a children's song, but at first not as the main voice. It resounds vaguely in the bassoon middle voice, and this stresses its introductory character. In the second half of the little piece the children's song becomes the melody, but is immediately dissolved by the use of its final notes. The next little piece, set to a few spoken verses of Walt Whitman, is structurally a brief coda to the introduction, but contains the beginning of a lullaby that for the time being is left undeveloped.

The first little 'main movement' is an allegro assai accompanying a playground scene. The games are not illustrated, the music has the general character of a merry noise. Free from the constraint of following the picture in detail, it approximates the structure of a sonatina exposition, without development. A 'cantabile theme' stands out clearly.

The next little movement follows the picture more closely. The children are painting toys with great seriousness and diligence. The music imitates this attitude with a busy little fugato.

Then the children are shown dragging heavy stones. The music retains the fugato theme and makes it laborious by purely structural changes. In the end the children quarrel, and the music suggests the pushing gestures.

The longest sequence – almost four minutes – is a potpourri of game fragments. The task of the music is to introduce unity into this variety. It consists of an introduction, a children's song with three variations, and a coda. Here a form of autonomous music is applied exactly to the film.

In one of the following scenes, a dog is being washed. The dramatic purpose was to evoke the humming that often accompanies mechanical work, although none of the children actually hums. Thus the music is not drawn realistically from the event on the screen, but from the mode of behavior that is represented by it. Only a short introduction refers to the dog's resistance; the actual washing is accompanied by a children's song on the strings (pizzicato, quasi à la banjo) and clarinet; it is somewhat developed, and in the next strophe inverted. The dog shakes himself dry to a brisk coda.

Then the children are shown feeding tiny newborn mice. They display utmost care, and the music reflects their care, nothing else – it is a fast-moving, high-pitched, anxiously squeaking piece.

Scenes of ball games gradually lead to a group using a live horse as a model for painting. Here the playful regularity of the game is reflected by a playful canon on a children's song, which is constructed in such a way that it also synchronizes with the sequence of painting.

The final scene is a visit to a farm. The children are watching various animals, and here the music is pastoral in character; it is purely decorative, more related to the scenery than to the events. At the end, a farm laborer gives the children a ride in a tiny wagon attached to a tractor. The tractor is seen as an immense machine, and here the music loses all childish character, and associates itself with tanks and war, in contradiction to the pastoral scene; it becomes serious, gloomy, agitated, and the style of the preceding composition is completely altered.

In contrast to the suite-like character of the music for *The Children's Camp*, the music for *Nature Scenes* offered an occasion for more developed and complex solutions. It had more elbow room, because it had no action or any human elements of which it had to take cognizance. On the other hand, the absence of any traces of dramatic continuity necessitated the composer's clinging to articulate musical forms. This naturally created the danger of unrelatedness – the music once unleashed might ignore everything but itself and become too pretentious. This danger was met by a composition that followed every detail of the picture sequence and changing camera angle, while fully preserving the formal independence of the music. The autonomy of the music was balanced by an attempt to achieve the exactitude of an animated cartoon in the synchronized treatment of single visual elements. The specific musical forms were made to correspond to the picture by the precision of their details. This is not formalistic, idle self-indulgence: every feature film still contains actual or virtual nature scenes with moods underscored by leitmotif padding. It seemed particularly important to point the way for more adequate solutions.

Five major musical forms were employed: the invention, the chorale prelude, the scherzo with trio, the étude, and the sonata finale. The composer tried to complicate his task by the use of the twelve-tone technique. Every element of the picture, for instance the collapse of an iceberg or the movement of a ship whose bow plows through ice floes, was thus subject to several requirements. As a concrete element of the musical form it had to have an independent musical meaning; it had to be 'attuned' to the twelve-tone system without sounding mechanical; it had to be structurally synchronized with the film, distinct, utterly precise.

Regarding the forms the following may be noted. The idea of the invention, the constant use of the theme in different tonal positions, is stimulated by the picture that shows the formation of a glacier – the theme – in varying perspectives, on various levels, so to speak. The chorale prelude is composed over a sustained *cantus firmus.* The étude is scored for two solo violins with orchestra accompaniment; the étude-like movement that runs through is a 'stylized' blizzard. The sonata exposition represents rigid glaciers, which collapse during the development; the recapitulation shows the result of the collapse – a bay filled with fragments of ice.

The scoring was conceived in accordance with the 'coldness' of the nature scenes. In addition to a normal chamber orchestra (flute, oboe, clarinet, bassoon, horn, trumpet, trombone, percussion, solo string quartet, and solo double-bass) an electric piano and novachord were used. The electrical instruments were not added for harmonic padding, as is usually done in the studios, but were treated soloistically. Sometimes there were real two-voice duets between them, accompanied by the orchestra. The coldness and sharpness of their 'manner,' such as trills, mordents, appoggiaturas, chain trills, were fully exploited.

The solutions attempted for the *Newsreels* were diametrically opposite ones. Utmost freedom from formal structures was sought; the music unreservedly adjusted itself to the picture, and the resultant form was that of the improvisation. The terror of a city bombed from the air – incidentally, it is utterly problematic whether music should be used for such documentary scenes, yet this is unavoidable under present-day conditions – resists treatment by autonomous musical forms. In so far as there is form in this instance, it is one contained in the picture itself. Countless details are shown, often lasting only a second each, which represent the many aspects of terror. The music follows along, constantly varies its character, does not give itself time for any contemplation, and is tied together only through contrasts.

Regarding the *Feature Film Sequences,* the task was to test various musical solutions for the same scene. Several scores were composed for each sequence, and each score was based on a different musico-dramatic idea. On the one hand, this procedure was suggested by the extraneous fact that the sequences were part of pictures for which the music already existed, so that any solution was actually an alternate solution; on the other, it was adopted for objective considerations. A feature film in which every moment has or should have a 'meaning' permits a far wider range of dramatic interpretation and a greater variety of possible attitudes toward such meanings than a nature scene that shows facts without trying to be meaningful. The purpose was to gauge the whole range of these dramatic possibilities.

A relatively long sequence from *Grapes of Wrath* begins with the wind blowing against deserted houses in the Dust Bowl region. It drives the dust that has driven away the farmers, as well as papers, old tin cans, refuse – the only traces left by the inhabitants. From a formal musical standpoint, the scene is introductory (23 seconds); it leads to a figurative 'colon,' which opens the first important musical sequence – the westward migration of the Joad family in an overloaded jalopy.

Musically this scene was approached from three different angles. First, sound effects without music were tried, the representation of the natural sounds of the picture. Then, a larghetto introduction voicing the despair expressed by the scene, pointing at it, as if to say: 'Just look at this!' Stressing of the meaning leads away from imitation of the events – there is no wind in the score, nor any sound track. The wind is only seen, and the effect of desertion is doubly strong. Finally, the orchestra reproduced the wind. Great emphasis was placed on the brilliance of the musical effect – the natural wind had to be surpassed, 'improved,' if the musical wind was to have any function at all. At the same time care was taken to achieve the utmost synchronization of the music with the tiniest details of the picture. In musical terms, however, the wind was an 'accompaniment system,' which carried a fragmentary melody for flute, and this melody 'expressed' the scene, just as did the second solution, although more lyrically. This third solution seemed the most adequate. Still other solutions are conceivable – for instance, aggressive ones, which would conceive the scene as a social catastrophe and voice a protest against it.

The contrast between music 'about' an event, from which it emphasizes its difference, and music that draws its impulses from the event in question defines the possible fundamental attitudes of music toward the motion picture, but admits manifold variations. These two attitudes are interrelated, productive of one another, not mechanically opposed. For instance, the naturalistic synchronized solution of the scene discussed here (the western trip of the Joad family) becomes a 'stylization' precisely because the music follows the trip in every detail; because the imitation is achieved by purely musical means, the consistent use of which gives birth to a specific formal principle. The stubborn imitation of the picture by the music is transformed into expression, that of intensive overcoming of resistance. The resultant 'character piece' could even be played in a concert. However, the opposite solution, one that takes its 'distance' from the film, solves a problem that was raised when the film was performed: the sight of the wretched jalopy loaded down with the poor belongings of the family was often greeted with laughter. Therefore, in the second solution, the music underscores the hopeless human struggle against the natural catastrophe, and before this wretched scene the listener's attention was focused on the family's will to hold out and survive the disaster.

Detailed Analysis of a Sequence

To illustrate the composing work done on the project, we give a detailed musical analysis of one sequence. It is part of the score to *Fourteen Ways of Describing Rain* (op. 70), which, as the richest and most complete of all those written under the auspices of the project, offers the most appropriate material for such an analysis. It is composed in the twelve-tone style, for the same ensemble of instruments that Arnold Schönberg (to whom the 'Rain' score is dedicated) used in his *Pierrot Lunaire* – flute, clarinet, violin (alternating with viola), cello, and piano. The task was to test the most advanced resources and the corresponding complex composing technique in their relation to the motion picture. The picture about the rain seemed particularly suitable for this because of its experimental character and the lyrical quality of many of its details, despite its thoroughly objective treatment. Every conceivable type of musico-dramatic solution was considered, from the simplest naturalism of synchronized detail painting to the most extreme contrast effects, in which music 'reflects' rather than follows a picture. The score consists of fourteen pieces, some loosely juxtaposed, and some structurally knit together. At the beginning and at the end there is a cadenza-like 'monogram.'

The second piece has been chosen for analysis (see pages 107–15). The picture shows the wind at the beginning of the rain. The dramatic concept of the sequence is extremely simple – precise and synchronized imitation of the picture events – but the musical resources are quite differentiated.

Measures 43 and 44 accompany a panorama showing clouds over the city and a weak wind that is beginning to blow. Measure 45 accompanies the picture of a detail – branches of a tree shaken by the wind. The music intones a recurrent chorale-like phrase recognizable by its triplet ending, to which the flute, clarinet, and cello join, while a violin figure, with trills almost like a faint noise, reproduces the wind.

In measures 45 and 46, the shaking of the boughs is translated into an incidental piano phrase, which is also important for the piece as a whole, and which, from a formal musical point of view, has the significance of the conclusion of a chorale stanza. Thus the form of the picture determined the musical form down to the smallest detail.

During measures 47 to 52 the picture is again panoramic. The wind is stronger, its effects can be seen in details: The music continues the first chorale phrase and expands the stanza to four measures, while the violin figure, as in the traditional chorale prelude, starts before the *cantus firmus.*

In measure 49 the chorale theme is taken over by the violin, and the figure representing the wind by the flute; the underlying motif has now been varied considerably. In measure 51, for the close-up of the effects of a gust of wind, the incidental piano phrase is resumed, and in 52 combined with the wind – the picture shows a gust of wind striking an awning. This picture motif continues during the third entrance of the chorale, measures 53 to 56, in the form of a violent outburst of the violin in its highest register, which, in relation to the first two, is like an 'aftersong.' The complex rhythm of the accompanying piano and cello reproduces the syncopated, gust-like rhythm of the picture.

The following little musical segment (measures 51 to 62) accompanies short scenes such as fallen leaves floating on a pond. The music is transitional in character, not unlike a flute cadenza. The wind motif, previously developed by the cello and transformed into a scale figure, is enlarged by the violin as a 'remnant,' as in the classical resolution of a motif, and thus logically continues the phrase described as 'aftersong.' The purpose of this procedure is to let abrupt contrasts grow out of one another and mediate them, without softening them.

Measure 63 corresponds to an important articulation in the picture: the first drops of rain are falling. Their drastically simple reproduction by means of coupled piano seconds results in a new theme that dominates the rest of the sequence. But it is accompanied by the chorale half notes in the clarinet and cello and then by the wind motif in the violin, while the cello takes over the new theme in pizzicato. At measure 70 it returns to the piano and is resolved in single quarter notes.

At measure 73 the raindrops have stopped and the pond with the floating leaves reappears on the screen. Accordingly the music goes back to the fragment of the flute cadenza, but divides it among the clarinet, flute, and violin. The violin once again leads it to a 'motif resolution' (measure 76).

Beginning with measure 77 a clear conclusion effect is produced. The screen shows a gray motionless sky overcast with rain clouds. The music, high above underlying harmonies, as though standing still, is a violin melody whose half notes are again reminiscent of the chorale figure. The peculiar brooding character of the passage is achieved by the way it is orchestrated. Cello and piano are in unison, but in such a way that the effect is a special coloring of the sound, not its reinforcement.

At measure 81 rain for the first time begins to fall thick and fast. The music hurries to the end. It picks up the piano theme of measure 63, but it no longer has time for any 'filigree work' and it flows almost without a pause in simple motion. The accompaniment, except for the rest of the deep harmonies that fades out soon, is a noise-like tremolo of the violin. In the two last measures the cello adds a suggestion of the chorale figure.

The form of the sequence does not fall under any of the usual categories. The recurring intonations of the melody in half notes are reminiscent of a chorale prelude; the equally recurring violin figures, of an étude. But neither of the two patterns corresponds to the actual form of the sequence, whose spirit rather approximates a sonata exposition, although the type of organization of the latter is not adopted externally. In chapter 6 it was pointed out that features such as principal themes, transitions, secondary themes, closing themes, or thematic resolutions, should be liberated from the formal pattern and made independent. Here an attempt was made in this direction. Thus the 'aftersong' in the first main section (measures 53 to 56) clearly has the character of a closing theme, of the fulfilment of a thematic development that actually has not preceded it. Also, the ending that starts with measure 81 has the effect of hurrying a detailed process to its conclusion, although such a process has not taken place. Such effects are made possible because the details of the classical sonata technique, especially those pertaining to the utmost motif economy and permanent variation, are retained, while the traditional architecture is replaced with the form of the picture.

Finally, the economy of the musical resources should be noted. Despite the prevailing filigree chamber-music texture of the composition, everything superfluous, everything that is not absolutely needed for the exposition of the musical idea, has been avoided. Even in this small quintet group, all the instruments play simultaneously only at rare moments. Such economy of means is particularly advisable in cinema music, which should avoid all superfluities.

Counter-Example

In order to see the foregoing analysis in its proper perspective, it is necessary to compare the composing procedure just described to the prevailing practice. For the sake of fairness, the contrasting example is not taken from the domain of commercial music, but from Eisenstein's book, where it is cited as a model of proper musical treatment according to the author's aesthetic theories. It is a short piece by Prokofiev, written to accompany a sequence from *Alexander Nevsky*.

The piece was obviously intended to be completely subordinated to the picture, without any independent musical requirements. Therefore our task is to analyze it from a purely dramatic functional point of view, not a musical one.

The underlying idea is that of similarity, not contrast. Eisenstein constructs diagrams of 'the picture rhythm' and the musical 'movement,' and considers the two identical. 'Now let us collate the two graphs,' he writes. 'What do we find? Both graphs of movement correspond absolutely, that is, we find a complete correspondence between the movement of the music and the movement of the eye over the lines of the plastic composition. In other words, exactly the same motion lies at the base of both the musical and the plastic structures.'[1]

In chapter 5 we have shown that the identification of musical and picture rhythms is questionable, because in plastic arts the concept of rhythm is largely metaphorical. This becomes manifest in the present case: Eisenstein's graphs refer to single shots, not to the time relation between them. Aside from this general consideration, the inadequacy of such analogies can be shown in detail with regard to Eisenstein's examples. Eisenstein's graphs are supposed to prove that the actual movement of the music is similar to the picture sequence. What they prove in reality is that there is similarity between the *notation* of the music and the sequence. But the notation is already the fixation of the actual musical movement, the static image of a dynamic phenomenon. The similarity between the music and the picture is indirect, suggested by the graphic fixation of the music; it cannot be perceived directly, and for that reason cannot fulfil a dramatic function.

For instance, shot No. V shows an avalanche. The music (see measure 9) imitates the steeply sloping rocks by descending dissolved triads that actually have the appearance of a precipitously falling curve in the notation. But the fall occurs in time, while the steeply sloping rock is seen unchanged from the first to the last note. Since the spectator does not read the notation but hears the music, it is quite impossible for him to associate the sequence of notes with the sloping rock. And he is even less likely to do so because the dissolved triad is such a conventional and worn-out phrase that the listener has not the slightest urge to connect it with a heroic scene. The musical formula used here is so inconsequential that it might relate to anything or nothing at all. Whether it is really necessary to have musical illustrations of steep rocks depends on the underlying plan. But if it is attempted, the motif should at least be so clear that no doubt is left concerning the relation between the music and the picture.

A further objection concerns the development of the sequence and the music. If Eisenstein's thesis of a correspondence between the two is accepted, the musical development would have to match that of the motion picture. The music then should distinguish between panoramic views and close-ups, as has been shown in the analysis of the rain sequence, and developing dramatic events should be reflected in specifically musical developments. The task here is to avoid having the music – which is by nature, dynamic – overstep the mark, as against the less mobile visual event. Paradoxically, the very opposite takes place in the Prokofiev piece: the picture moves on while the music marks time. For instance there is a clear difference in the stage of development between the first three shots, which show details, and the fourth shot which is a general view of a battle line with two flags. But measures 5 to 8 literally repeat measures 1 to 4, and Eisenstein's repeated recommendations in regard to the correspondence between the picture sequence and the musical movement here completely go unheeded. In shot No. IV two flags are symbolically represented by 4 eighths (measure 8).

Unfortunately, the same eighth notes have previously appeared in measure 4, shot No. II, which does not show any flag, although there is a lance in it, which one of the warriors brandishes in the air. If static picture details are to be so pedantically translated into music, the pedantry should at least be consistent, not practised one moment and forgotten the next.

Beginning with shot No. VI, the character of the picture changes; it progresses from medium shots to close-ups. Gradually people detach themselves from the background, a rudimentary plot begins to appear. The music, however, does not pay any attention to this, it repeats its highly simple tone pattern, on the same g sharp that it has grazed in the third measure and definitely reached in the tenth. Prokofiev follows the neo-classical principle of impassivity, of unemotional repetition of musical pattern as opposed to progressive action, and Eisenstein, quite unconcerned with the true nature of this musical style, gives it an interpretation, after the fashion of program music, that is absolutely unjustified by the musical content.

However, Prokofiev himself does not remain true to his neo-classical principle, but obliges Eisenstein, in so far as his rigidly repeated fundamental pattern is supposed to represent a musical mood of agitation, the very opposite of rigidity. Thus a contradiction results between the fundamental musical pattern he has chosen and his treatment of it. The impassivity would have been genuine if it had been exactly contrasted with the agitated picture, as is the case, for instance, in some of Stravinsky's ballet scenes. But Prokofiev goes only half way, and what is achieved is neither neo-classical impassivity nor romantic program music, but merely a blurred and inexact relation between picture and music. The basic patterns and the musical graphs are similar, but the development of the music and that of the picture are quite dissimilar and unrelated – in fact, the music does not develop at all.

Finally, one of Eisenstein's fundamental misconceptions should be pointed out. He transfers his whole discussion to a sphere of high-sounding aesthetic arguments,[2] which is completely irrelevant to the harmless piece that Prokofiev without much effort wrote for the sequence in question. Eisenstein speaks of this piece and its relation to the picture as though he were dealing with the most difficult problems of abstract

From Eisenstein's *The Film Sense*, p. 189. Courtesy of Harcourt, Brace and Company.

painting, with reference to which phrases such as steep curves, green counterpoints to blue themes, or structural unity, have been used only too frequently. He uses heavy artillery to shoot sparrows. The piece in question so completely follows the beaten tracks of good old cinema music that to speak of its 'structure' does not make sense. Tremolos are supposed to suggest a suspense that no one any longer attributes to them; a syncopated eighth-note rhythm that has long since become ineffective is supposed to be 'ragged,' and a sequence of quarter notes rising to triads is supposed to 'threaten,' while actually it does not even leave the safe circle of the surrounding harmonies. The music is that of the old *Kinothek*, only the terminology is that of Kandinsky's manifestoes.

Not even a provincial conductor would do it so:

Example from Schweitzer (p. 156).

FOURTEEN WAYS TO DESCRIBE RAIN

Hanns Eisler

In honor of Arnold Schönberg's seventieth birthday
No. 3

APPENDIX

112

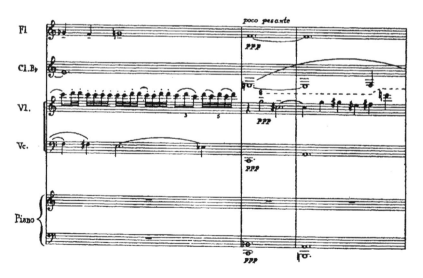

Notes

New Introduction

1 Brecht/Eisler, 'Das Einheitsfrontlied' (1934).
2 Adorno, *Aesthetic Theory*, trans. C. Lenhardt (London: Routledge, 1984), p. 1.
3 Albrecht Betz, *Hanns Eisler Political Musician*, trans. Bill Hopkins (Cambridge: Cambridge University Press, 1982). See also Manfred Grabs (ed.), *Hanns Eisler: A Rebel in Music* (Berlin: Seven Seas Publishing, 1979). Heinz Josef Herbort, 'Hanns Eisler – Porträt eines Nonkonformisten', *Die Zeit*, 14 June 1968; George Lukacs, 'In Memoriam Hanns Eisler', *Alternative*, 69, 1969; and David Drew, 'Eisler and the Polemic Symphony', *The Listener*, 4 January 1962.
4 Leo Löwenthal, *Critical Theory and Frankfurt Theorists* (New Brunswick: Transaction 1989) p. 53. See also Martin Jay's remarkably lucid yet concise introductory text, *Adorno* (London: Fontana, 1984); Fredric Jameson, 'Introduction to T.W. Adorno', *Salmagundi*, 10–11 (Fall 1969–Winter 1970); Kurt Oppens *et al.*: *Über Theodor W. Adorno* (Frankfurt am Main: Suhrkamp, 1968); Gillian Rose, *The Melancholy Science* (London: Macmillan, 1978); and Leo Löwenthal, 'Recollections of Theodor W. Adorno', in *Critical Theory and Frankfurt Theorists*.
5 See Martin Jay, *Adorno*, note 22, p. 168.
6 See Adorno, *Alban Berg* (Cambridge: Cambridge University Press, 1991).
7 The Institute's view of 'Critical Theory' is probably best summed up in Horkheimer's 1937 article, 'Traditional and Critical Theory', reprinted in *Critical Theory: Selected Essays*, trans. Matthew J. O'Connell *et al.* (New York: Herder & Herder, 1972). Martin Jay's *The Dialectical Imagination*. (London: Heinemann, 1973) is still the most accomplished history of the Institute. Leo

Löwenthal's 'The Institute of Social Research', in *An Unmastered Past* (Berkeley: University of California Press, 1987), is an illuminating first-hand account which neatly clarifies many common misconceptions. For further background information, see David Held, *Introduction to Critical Theory* (London: Hutchinson, 1980); Eugene Lunn, *Marxism and Modernism* (London: Verso, 1985); Rolf Wiggershaus, *The Frankfurt School* (Cambridge: Polity, 1994); and Martin Jay, *Permanent Exiles* (New York: Columbia University Press, 1986). For examples of the Institute's work, see Andrew Arato/Eike Gebhardt (eds), *The Essential Frankfurt School Reader* (New York: Continuum, 1990) and Stephen Eric Bronner/Douglas MacKay Kellner (eds), *Critical Theory and Society: A Reader* (London: Routledge, 1989).

8 A position Adorno defended most precisely in his essay 'Resignation', reprinted in *The Culture Industry*, ed. J.M. Bemstein (London: Routledge, 1991).

9 Adorno, *Minima Moralia*, trans. E.F.N. Jephcott (London: NLB, 1974) p. 86.

10 Adorno, *Minima Moralia*, p. 80. For a helpful discussion of Adorno's stylistic techniques, see Gillian Rose, *The Melancholy Science*, chapter 2, and Samuel M. Weber, 'Translating the Untranslatable', in Adorno, *Prisms* (Cambridge, Mass.: MIT, 1981).

11 Bertolt Brecht, *Flüchtlingsgespräche* (Frankfurt a.M.: Suhrkamp, 1961) p. 112.

12 See Helmut F. Pfanner, *Exile in New York: German and Austrian Writers after 1933* (Detroit: Wayne State University Press, 1983).

13 Adorno, *Minima Moralia*, p. 33.

14 Löwenthal, *Critical Theory and Frankfurt Theorists*, p. 64.

15 Adorno, 'Scientific Experiences of a European Scholar in America', in Donald Fleming/Bemard Bailyn (eds), *The Intellectual Migration: Europe and America, 1930–1960* (Cambridge, Mass.: Harvard University Press, 1969), p. 338. One should resist the temptation to accept the common view of Adorno as 'anti-American': as he makes clear in this essay, in America he discerned 'a potential for real generosity that is seldom to be found in old Europe . . . There is an inherent impulse in American life toward peaceableness, good-naturedness, and generosity, in the sharpest contrast to the dammed-up malice and envy that exploded in Germany between 1933 and 1945', pp. 367–8.

16 Paul Lazarsfeld, 'An Episode in the History of Social Research: A Memoir', in Fleming/Bailyn, *The Intellectual Migration*, p. 301.

17 Brecht, *Arbeitsjournal* (Frankfurt a.M.: Suhrkamp, 1973), p. 498.

18 *Ibid.*, p. 422.

19 Eric Bentley, *The Brecht Memoir* (Manchester: Carcanet, 1989), p. 16.

20 The *première*, with Laughton in the title role, took place at the Coronet Theatre in Beverly Hills on 31 July 1947. See Simon Callow, *Charles Laughton: A Difficult Actor* (London: Methuen, 1987), pp. 178–96, and Barbara Learning, *Orson Welles* (London: Weidenfeld & Nicolson, 1985), pp. 324–8.

NOTES

21 Thomas Mann, *Letters of Thomas Mann 1989–1955*, trans. Richard and Clara Winston (Berkeley: University of California Press, 1970), p. 362. Adorno is the unnamed source of the reflections on Beethoven in chapter VIII of the novel, and appears as the Devil in chapter XXV. See Thomas Mann, *The Story of a Novel*, trans. Richard and Clara Winston (New York: Knopf, 1961).

22 Salka Viertel, *The Kindness of Strangers* (New York: Holt, Rinehart and Winston, 1969), pp. 257–9.

23 Charles Chaplin, *My Autobiography* (New York: Simon & Schuster, 1964), p. 452.

24 Eisler, Letter to Clifford Odets, 23 April 1946, cited in Betz, *Hanns Eisler Political Musician*, p. 195.

25 Adorno/Eisler, *Composing for the Films*, p. 95.

26 *Ibid.*, p. 111.

27 *Ibid.*, p. 91.

28 *Ibid.*, p. 113.

29 *Ibid.*, pp. 12–14.

30 See Salka Viertel, *The Kindness of Strangers*, pp. 207–8.

31 John Baxter, *The Hollywood Exiles* (London: Macdonald and Janes, 1976), p. 219.

32 Adorno wrote to Kracauer on 22 December 1942. See Martin Jay, 'Adorno and Kracauer: Notes on a Troubled Friendship', in *Permanent Exiles*, pp. 217–36, and Adorno, 'The Curious Realist: On Siegfried Kracauer', in *Notes to Literature*, vol. 2, trans. Shierry Weber Nicholsen (New York: Columbia University Press, 1992) pp. 58–75. Kracauer's own work on movies includes *From Caligari to Hitler* (Princeton: Princeton University Press, 1960) and *Theory of Film* (New York: Oxford University Press, 1960). For a discussion of his earlier German writings, see Heide Schlüpmann, 'Phenomenology of Film: On Siegfried Kracauer's Writings of the 1920s', *New German Critique* 40 (Winter 1987), pp. 97–114.

33 Adorno, 'Scientific Experiences of a European Scholar in America', Fleming/Bailyn, *The Intellectual Migration*, p. 344.

34 *Ibid.*, p. 347.

35 *Ibid.*, pp. 350–51.

36 The text was written during the period 1941–1944, and was published in 1947. The original subtitle, omitted from the English translation, was 'Philosophical Fragments'. Other members of the Institute made certain unacknowledged contributions to the text (see Löwenthal, *An Unmastered Past*, p. 211).

37 Adorno/Horkheimer: *Dialectic of Enlightenment*, trans. John Cumming (London: Verso, 1979), pp. 144–5.

38 Adorno, 'culture industry reconsidered', *The Culture Industry*, p. 87.

39 Adorno/Horkheimer, *Dialectic of Enlightenment*, p. 139.

40 *Ibid.*, p. 154.

41 See, for example, Tino Balio (ed.), *The American Film Industry* (Madison: University of Wisconsin Press, 1976).

42 Adorno. Quoted in Herbert Marcuse, *One Dimensional Man* (London: Ark, 1986), note 19, p. 99.

43 Adorno/Horkheimer, *Dialectic of Enlightenment*, p. 144.

44 Adorno, 'On the Fetish-Character in Music and the Regression of Listening' (1938), reprinted in Arato/Gebhardt, *The Essential Frankfurt School Reader*, pp. 270–99. *Ibid.*, p. 282. For background information on Adorno's sociology of music, see Harold Blumenfeld, 'Ad Vocem Adorno', *The Music Quarterly* 75, 4 (Winter 1991), pp. 263–84; Ronald Weitzman, 'An Introduction to Adorno's Music and Social Criticism', *Music and Letters* 52, (3 July 1971), pp. 287–98; W. V. Blomster, 'Sociology of Music: Adorno and Beyond', *Telos*, 28 (Summer 1976), pp. 81–112; and Max Paddison, *Adorno's Aesthetics of Music* (Cambridge: Cambridge University Press, 1993).

45 Adorno, 'On the Fetish-Character in Music and the Regression of Listening', *The Essential Frankfurt School Reader*, p. 282.

46 *Ibid.*, p. 281.

47 *Ibid.*, p. 281.

48 Adorno, *Introduction to the Sociology of Music* (New York: Seabury, 1976), p. 46.

49 Adorno, *Musikblätter des Anbruch*, (Vienna) 1925, p. 423. A similarly positive review, of the Piano Pieces op. 3, was written by Adorno for *Die Musik* (Stuttgart), July 1927, pp. 749f.

50 Eric Bentley's *The Brecht Memoir* (p. 15) notes that when Stalin dissolved the Comintern in 1943, Eisler 'bounded to the piano and "dissolved" his Comintern anthem in a succession of harmonies that made the original tune quite disappear'.

51 Adorno, *Aesthetic Theory*, p. 8.

52 Adorno, 'On the Social Situation of Music', *Telos*, 35 (Spring 1978), p. 130.

53 Adorno, *Aesthetic Theory*, p. 31.

54 Adorno, 'On the Social Situation of Music', p. 130.

55 Adorno, *Prisms*, trans. Samuel and Shierry Weber (Cambridge, Mass.: MIT, 1981), p. 166.

56 See Adorno, 'Commitment', in Arato/Gebhardt, *The Essential Frankfurt School Reader*, pp. 300–18.

57 Adorno, *Aesthetic Theory*, p. 344.

58 Brecht, quoted in Iring Fetscher, 'Bertolt Brecht and America', *Salmagundi*, 10–11 (Fall 1969–Winter 1970), p. 264.

59 Eisler, quoted from Hans Bunge, *Fragen Sie mehr über Brecht, Hanns Eisler im Gespräch* (Munich: Rogner & Bernhard, 1970), p. 189.

60 Löwenthal, 'Adorno and his Critics', *Critical Theory and Frankfurt Theorists*, p. 54.

61 *Ibid.*, pp. 55–6.
62 Adorno, 'Resignation', *The Culture Industry*, p. 174.
63 Adorno, *Aesthetic Theory*, p. 360.
64 Adorno/Eisler: *Composing for the Films*, p. ix.
65 *Ibid.*, p. 59.
66 *Ibid.*, pp. 8–9.
67 *Ibid.*, p. 6.
68 *Ibid.*, p. 9.
69 *Ibid.*, p. 12.
70 Adorno, *Introduction to the Sociology of Music*, p. 31.
71 Adorno/Eisler: *Composing for the Films*, pp. 20–23.
72 *Ibid.*, p. 121.
73 *Ibid.*, p. 37.
74 *Ibid.*, p. 108.
75 *Ibid.*, p. 120.
76 *Ibid.*, p. 132.
77 *Ibid.*, p. 32.
78 *Ibid.*, p. 23.
79 For information on this period, see Alvah Bessie, *Inquisition in Eden* (New York: Macmillan, 1965) and Larry Ceplair/Stephen Englund, *The Inquisition in Hollywood: Politics in the Film Community, 1930–1960* (Garden City, NY: Doubleday, 1980).
80 Quoted from Betz, *Hanns Eisler Political Musician*, p. 197.
81 *Los Angeles Examiner*, 26 April 1947.
82 *Hearings Regarding Hanns Eisler*, Washington 1947 (Government Printing Office) p. 25.
83 See, for example, Adorno's 'Transparencies on film' and 'Free time', both included in *The Culture Industry*. For secondary material on Adorno and film, see Thomas Andrae, 'Adorno on Film and Mass Culture', *Jump Cut* 20 (May 1979); Miriam Hansen, 'Introduction to Adorno, ''Transparencies on Film'' ' *New German Critique* 24/25 (Fall/Winter 1981–82); and Diane Waldman, 'Critical Theory and Film', *New German Critique* 12 (Fall 1977).
84 For Adorno's account of the multiple texts, see his *Gesammelte Schriften*, ed. Rolf Tiedemann, vol. 15 (Frankfurt a.M.: Suhrkamp, 1976), pp. 144–6. For an analysis of the original English version, see Philip Rosen, 'Adorno and Film Music: Theoretical Notes on *Composing for the Films*', *Yale French Studies* 60 (1980), pp. 157–82, and, for the controversy, Hanns Mayer, 'An Aesthetic Debate of 1951: Comment on a Text by Hanns Eisler', *New German Critique*, 2 (Spring, 1974), pp. 58–62, and Günter Mayer, 'Adorno und Eisler' in Otto Kolleritsch (ed.), *Adorno und die Musik* (Graz: Universal Edition, 1979), pp. 135–55.
85 Adorno, *Minima Moralia*, p. 209.

1. Prejudices and Bad Habits

1 A prominent Hollywood composer, in an interview quoted in the newspapers, declared that there is no fundamental difference between his methods of composing and Wagner's. He, too, uses the leitmotif.

2 As a matter of fact, the modern concept of melody made itself felt as early as within Viennese classicism. Nowhere does the historical character of this apparently natural concept become more manifest than in the famous Mozart critique by Hans Georg Naegeli, the Swiss contemporary of the Viennese classicists, which is now made accessible in a reprint edited by Willi Reich. Musical history generally recognizes as one of the greatest merits of Mozart that he introduced the element of cantability into the sonata form, particularly the complex of the second theme. This innovation, largely responsible for the musical changes that led to the crystallization of the later *Lied* melody, was by no means greeted enthusiastically in all quarters. To Naegeli, who was certainly narrow-minded and dogmatic but had rather articulate philosophical ideas about musical style, Mozart's synthesis of instrumental writing and cantability appeared about as shocking as advanced modern composition would to a popular-music addict of today. He blames Mozart, who is now regarded by the musical public as the utmost representative of stylistic purity, for lack of taste and style. The following passage is characteristic: 'His [Mozart's] genius was great but its defect, the overuse of contrast, was equally great. This was all the more objectionable in his case because he continuously contrasted the non-instrumental with the instrumental, cantability with the free play of tones. This was inartistic, as it is in all arts. As soon as continuous contrast becomes the main effect, the beautiful proportion of parts is necessarily neglected. This stylistic fault can be discovered in many of Mozart's works.' (Hans Georg Naegeli, *Von Bach zu Beethoven*, Benno Schwabe & Co., Basel, 1946, pp. 48–9.)

3 In the realm of motion pictures the term 'technique' has a double meaning that can easily lead to confusion. On the one hand, technique is the equivalent of an industrial process for producing goods: e.g., the discovery that picture and sound can be recorded on the same strip is comparable to the invention of the air brake. The other meaning of 'technique' is aesthetic. It designates the method by which an artistic intention can be adequately realized. While the technical treatment of music in sound pictures was essentially determined by the industrial factor, there was a need for music from the very beginning, because of certain aesthetic requirements. Thus far no clear-cut relation between the factors has been established, neither in theory nor in practice (Cf. ch. 5).

* Translated by N. G.

4 'By pseudo-individualization we mean endowing cultural mass production

with the halo of free choice or open market on the basis of standardization itself.' (T. W. Adorno, 'On Popular Music,' in *Studies in Philosophy and Social Science*, vol. IX, 1941, p. 25.)

2. Function and Dramaturgy

1　A remark of Goethe's confirms this. 'According to my father everyone should learn to draw, and for that reason he had great regard for Emperor Maximilian, who was said to have given explicit orders to that effect. He also more seriously urged me to practice drawing than music, which, on the other hand, he recommended to my sister, even keeping her at the piano for a good part of the day, in addition to her regular lessons.' *(Dichtung und Wahrheit,* Part I, Book IV.) The boy, visualized by the father as a representative of progress and enlightenment, is supposed to train his eye, while the girl, who represents historically outmoded domesticity and has no real share in public life and economic production, is confined to music, as was generally the case with young upper-class women in the nineteenth century, quite apart from the role of music throughout oriental society.

2　Cf. Ernst Kurth, *Musikpsychologie,* Berlin, 1931, pp. 116–36: e.g., 'There is not only the perceptual space that is drawn into musical expression from outside; there is also a space or inner listening, which is an autonomous musico-psychological phenomenon' (p. 134); or: 'The spatial impressions of music also claim their independence; it is essential ... that they should not arise by the detour of any perceptual image. They pertain to energetic processes, and are autogenous' (p. 135).

3　This perhaps helps to explain why modern music meets with so much greater resistance than modern painting. The ear clings to the archaic essence of music, while music itself is involved in the process of rationalization.

3. The New Musical Resources

1　It is worthy of note that certain features of the work of Alban Berg, whose late-romantic, expressionistic instrumental and operatic music is far removed from the motion-picture and the new 'functional' style, illustrate the prevalence in advanced music of objective tendencies in the sense of a rational construction which come close to the requirements of the motion picture. Berg thinks in terms of such exact mathematical proportions that the number of bars and thereby the duration of his compositions are determined in advance. It is as if he composed them with a stop watch in his hand. His operas, in which complex stage situations are often accompanied by complex musical forms, such as fugues, in order to make them articulate, strive toward a type of technical procedure that might be called a musical close-up.

2   The predominance of discords in the new musical language leads to the dissolution of tonality, for neither the separate harmonic incidents nor their functional connection and the harmonic structure of the whole can any longer be adequately represented in the pattern, however broadened, of traditional tonality. But this dissolution of tonality is furthered most by the objective formal structure of motion-picture music itself. This structure has a definite bearing upon harmony. With some exaggeration one might say that motion-picture music is driven to atonality because there is no room in it for the formally satisfactory expansion of tonality. To be sure, the individual harmonic incidents of the usual motion-picture music are almost without exception strictly tonal, or at most only 'seasoned' with dissonances. But the tonality remains one of single sounds and their most primitive sequences. The necessity of following cues, and of producing harmonic effects without regard for the requirements of harmonic development, obviously does not permit of really balanced modulation, broad, well-planned harmonic canvases; in brief, real tonality in the sense of the disposition of functional harmony over long stretches. And it is this, not the atoms of the triads or seventh chords, which constitutes tonal organization. What was said above concerning leitmotifs is in a higher sense true of the tonal principle itself. If one went backwards, that is to say, from the dramaturgically inevitable breaks and deviations of the composition, something like satisfactory tonal relationships might be achieved by means of extreme care and virtuosity in composition; but according to the prevailing practice, while the separate chords are banal and over-familiar, their interrelation is quite anarchistic and for the most part completely meaningless. True, the emancipation of tonality does not, according to the strictest criteria, facilitate the harmonic disposition, but at least it liberates the composer from the preoccupation of restoring the basic key and the selection of modulations, which are hardly ever consistent with the extra-musical requirements of the motion picture. Moreover, the dissonances have far greater mobility and adjustability, and unlike tonal chords which are derived from the pattern and need the restoration of the pattern for their own fulfilment do not require to the same degree unambiguous definite inevitable resolutions.

3   The extraordinary effectiveness of Stravinsky's earlier works can be partly explained by his renunciation of neo-romantic melodizing.

4. Sociological Aspects

1   Kurt London, *Film Music,* London, Faber and Faber, n.d., pp. 50–61.

2   Flaubert described this type as early as the middle of the nineteenth century: 'The singer Lagardy had a beautiful voice, more temperament than intelligence, more pathos than feeling. He was both a genius and a charlatan,

and in his nature there was as much of a barber as of a toreador.' (*Madame Bovary*.)

3 The violinist who stands while he conducts a café orchestra, the other members remaining seated.

4 London, op. cit. p. 43.

5 Kracauer, S., *Die Angestellten. Aus dem neuesten Deutschland*, Frankfurt, 1930. [*Die Angestellten* appeared more recently as volume five of Kracauer's *Schriften* (Frankfurt: Suhrkamp, 1971)].

6 This statement is not a sociological exaggeration, as can be seen from the following clause that is part of a typical Hollywood contract: 'All material composed, submitted, added or interpolated by the Writer pursuant to this agreement shall automatically become the property of the Corporation, which, for this purpose, shall be deemed the author thereof, the Writer acting entirely as the Corporation's employee.' The extent to which the composer renounces his artistic independence is shown in another passage of the same contract, according to which the writer grants to the corporation 'the right to use, adapt and change the same or any part thereof and to combine the same with other works of the Writer or of any other person to the extent that the Corporation may see fit, including the right to add to, subtract from, arrange, rearrange, revise and adapt such material in any Picture in any manner.' However, when the corporation wants to protect itself against possible breach of the contract by the composer, his music is suddenly endowed with the traditional dignity of a work of art. Thus, 'it is agreed that the services to be performed by the Writer pursuant to this agreement, and the rights and privileges granted to the Corporation by the Writer under the terms thereof, are of a special, unusual, extraordinary and intellectual character which gives them a peculiar value, the loss of which cannot be reasonably or adequately compensated for by damages in a lawsuit, and that a breach by the Writer of any of the provisions contained in this agreement will cause the Corporation irreparable injury and damage.' The disproportion between the omnipotence of the corporation and the impotence of those who sell their services to it could not be more trenchantly expressed.

7 Cf. T. W. Adorno, who wrote in 1929 concerning the threadbare operatic melodies used in Naples as accompaniments to motion pictures that they could 'not be perceived as music by the spectators, but exist musically only for the picture ... It comes to comfort the picture because the picture is mute, and lulls it gently into the darkness of the theater even when it assumes the gestures of passion. It is not addressed to the spectator who notices it only when the picture drifts far away from him, separated by the abyss of mere space.' (*Anbruch*, vol. XI, p. 337)

5. Elements of Aesthetics

1 Hegel, *Vorlesungen über die Ästhetik,* W. W. 1. Band, 1. Abteilung, ed. Hotho, Berlin, 1842, p. 180.

2 Sergei Eisenstein, *The Film Sense,* New York, 1942, p. 157.

3 Ibid. p. 161. The example Eisenstein gives for the interpretation of the inner movement of the Barcarolle is not convincing. In the Silly Symphony *Birds of a Feather* (1921), Walt Disney related that piece to 'a Peacock whose tail shimmers ''musically'' and who looks into the pool to find there the identical contours of its opalescent tail feathers, shimmering upside down. All the approachings, recedings, ripples, reflections and opalescence that came to mind as a suitable essence to be drawn from the Venetian scenes, have been preserved by Disney in the same relation to the music's movement: the spreading tail and its reflection approach each other and recede according to the nearness of the flourished tail to the pool – the tail feathers are themselves waving and shimmering – and so on.' However, Disney's pretty idea does not imply the direct transformation of one medium into another. The transformation is indirect, literary in character, based on the generally accepted premise that this popular piece is associated with water, gondolas, and therefore with Venetian opalescent effects. The intention here is to show by the interpolation of a concept that the colors of a bird can symbolize Venice. The idea of the playful interchangeability of different elements of reality as well as subtle irony with regard to Venice, which is likened, in its picturesqueness, to a peacock, are ingredients inseparable from the effect of Disney's interpretation. This effect is certainly legitimate, but the doctrine of inner movement does not even begin to account for it. It is a highly sophisticated effect and Eisenstein's purely formal, literal interpretation misses the point. – This example shows the inadequacy of formal-aesthetic discussions of even highly stylized, nonrealistic pictures; with regard to more realistic films, this inadequacy is even more flagrant.

4 Ibid. p. 168.

5 London, op. cit. p. 73.

6 'Two film pieces of any kind, placed together, inevitably combine into a new concept, a new quality, arising out of that juxtaposition.' (Eisenstein, op. cit. p. 4.) This applies not only to the clash of heterogeneous pictorial elements, but also to that of music and picture, particularly when they are not assimilated to each other.

7 'What is stunted in the age of technical reproducibility, is the aura of the work of art.' The aura is 'the unrepeatable, single impression of something presented as remote, however close it may be. To follow with one's eyes a mountain chain on a summer afternoon or a bough that casts its shadow on one resting under it – is to breathe the aura of those mountains, of that

bough.' The aura is 'bound with the here and now, there can be no copy of it.' (Walter Benjamin, 'L'oeuvre d'art à l'époque de sa reproduction mécanisée', in *Zeitschrift für Sozialforschung,* V., Paris, 1936–7, pp. 40 ff.) [The English version of the essay is 'The Work of Art in the Age of Mechanical Reproduction', in Benjamin's *Illuminations* (London: Fontana, 1992), pp. 215ff.]

8   The quotation is from Franz Werfel, 'Ein Sommernachtstraum, Ein Film von Shakespeare und Reinhardt,' in *Neues Wiener Journal,* quoted in LU, 15 Nov. 1935.

9   Eisenstein is aware of the materialistic potentialities of the principle of montage: the juxtaposition of heterogeneous elements raises them to the level of consciousness and takes over the function of theory. This is probably the meaning of Eisenstein's formulation: 'Montage has a realistic significance when the separate pieces produce, in juxtaposition, the generality, the synthesis of one's theme' (op. cit. p. 30). The real achievement of montage is always interpretation.

10 Kurt London makes the following illuminating remark: 'It [motion-picture music] began not as a result of any artistic urge, but from the dire need of something which would drown the noise made by the projector. For in those times there was as yet no sound-absorbent walls between the projection machine and the auditorium. This painful noise disturbed visual enjoyment to no small extent. Instinctively cinema proprietors had recourse to music, and it was the right way, using an agreeable sound to neutralize one less agreeable.' (London, op. cit. p. 28.) This sounds plausible enough. But there remains the question, why should the sound of the projector have been so unpleasant? Hardly because of its noisiness, but rather because it seemed to belong to that uncanny sphere which anyone who remembers the magic-lantern performances can easily evoke. The grating, whirring sound actually had to be 'neutralized,' 'appeased,' not merely muted. If one reconstructed a cinema booth of the type used in 1900 and made the projector work in the audience room, more might be learned about the origin and meaning of motion-picture music than from extensive research. The experience in question is probably a collective one akin to panic, and it involves the flash-like awareness of being a helpless inarticulate mass given over to the power of a mechanism. Such an impulse is easily rationalized, for instance, as fear of fire. It is basically the feeling that something may befall a man even if he be 'many.' This is precisely the consciousness of one's own mechanization.

11 Cf. T. W. Adorno: 'The Radio Symphony', in *Radio Research 1941,* New York, 1941, pp. 110–39.

12 This could be checked by empirical methods. If the audience of a motion picture were given a questionnaire after the performance and asked to state which scenes were accompanied by music and which were not, and to

characterize this music in a general way, it is likely that hardly any of them would be able to answer these questions with approximate correctness, not even musicians, unless they came to see the picture for professional reasons.

13 *Phänomenologie des Geistes*, ed. Lasson, 2. Auflage, Leipzig, 1921, p. 60.

6. The Composer and the Movie-Making Process

1 Cf. the 'closing' almost coda-like modification of the introductory adagio in the C-minor fantasy in its reprise. It differs from its first form more than does any sonata recapitulation of Mozart.

2 The word 'setting' is used as a translation of the German *Satz* in a specific meaning for which there is no precise English equivalent. It refers to the way the 'texture' of a composition, how it is 'set,' takes into account the conditions of its actual realization in sound, e.g., the invention of themes out of the specific character of an instrument, the choice of high or low sonorities, the distance between different simultaneous parts, contrapuntal complexity or simplicity according to the requirement of making every musical idea clear and understandable. In other words, 'setting' is the way in which the necessities of scoring express themselves in the structure of the music, and will be used in this sense throughout the following discussion.

7. Suggestions and Conclusions

1 See p. 121, fn. 4.

2 More generally, the question must at least be raised whether the technification of the work of art does not lead inevitably to the ultimate elimination of art. 'Art still has a limitation within itself, and therefore passes into higher forms of conscious activity ... We no longer hold art to be the highest mode in which truth acquires existence ... With the progress of culture, every nation reaches a time in which art points beyond itself ... Such a time is our own.' (Hegel, *Vorlesungen ueber die Aesthetik*, vol. I, 1842, p. 132.) In the second part of his *Aesthetics* Hegel discusses the tendency to self-dissolution historically inherent in art, and connects it with the progress of civilization. The following passage is directly relevant to the problems of the motion picture and aesthetic planning: 'For the modern artist, to be bound to a particular content and a manner appropriate only to a given material, is a thing of the past, Thereby art has become a free instrument, which he can apply equally with regard to every content of whatever nature, according to the measure of his subjective skill.' (Ibid. vol. II, p. 232.)

3 The problem of the comical potentialities of music is inseparable from the meaning of the motion picture itself. This is magnificently shown in the

pictures of the Marx Brothers, who demolish an opera set as though to express allegorically the philosophic insight into the disintegration of the opera itself ... or smash a grand piano and seize the framework and strings as a sample of the harp of the future ... The main reason for the tendency of music to become comical in the present phase, is that something so completely useless should be practised with all the visible signs of strenuous serious work. The fact that music is alien to industrious people reveals their alienation with regard to one another, and the awareness of this alienation vents itself in laughter.' (T. W. Adorno, 'Ueber den Fetisch-charakter in der Musik und die Regression des Hörens', in *Zeitschrift für Sozialforschung*, VII, 1938, p. 353.) [The English translation is 'On the Fetish-Character in Music and the Regression of Listening', in Andrew Arato/Eike Gebhardt (eds) *The Essential Frankfurt School Reader* (New York: Continuum, 1990) p. 297.

Appendix

1 Sergei Eisenstein. *The Film Sense*, New York, 1942, p. 178.
2 Eisenstein also shows a tendency toward uncritical adoption of certain results of musical semi-erudition, such as are found in Albert Schweitzer's well-known and highly overrated book on Bach.

'How far he [Bach] will venture to go in music is shown in the Christmas cantata, *Christum wir sollen loben schon.* The text of the aria *Johannis freudenvolles Sprlngen erkannte dich mein Jesus schon* refers to the passage in the Gospel of St. Luke, ''And it came to pass that when Elisabeth heard Mary's greeting the babe leaped in the womb.'' Bach's music is simply a series of violent convulsions.' (Eisenstein, l.c. p. 162 f.) In describing the passages cited as convulsions, Schweitzer forgets that such passages belong to the general musical resources of the whole Bach period, that they are found in hundreds of his works with entirely different connotations, without necessarily expressing embryos leaping in their mothers' wombs. To give the effect of leaping, one would have to perform the music in a 'leaping' way, and even the most ambitious provincial time beater would hardly indulge in such romanticism.

Index